Innocent Victims

Innocent Victims

Helping Children Through The Trauma of Divorce

Thomas Whiteman Ph.D.

Copyright © 1991 by Thomas Whiteman

All rights reserved.

For information, address:
Fresh Start
751 North Wayne Avenue
Wayne, PA 19087

ISBN 0-938289-03-9

Library of Congress Cataloging in Publication Data is
available.

Printed in the United States of America.

DEDICATION

This book is dedicated to the more than five hundred single parents and their children, whose stories provided the impetus for this book. It is their stories and their experiences which will be shared here, and it was for their sake that this book was written. It is hoped that our combined efforts will help to alleviate some of the negative consequences of divorce for the tens of thousands of families in crisis who will pick up this book and read their stories.

Contents

Introduction

This book has grown out of an obvious need. A need which is evidenced in our city streets, our jails, and among our homeless; but also in our private schools, our churches, and in the nicest of neighborhoods. The need has been dramatically felt by all those who have watched as their children have reacted to the disruption of the family. It is the need for early intervention in the lives of those who are experiencing the break-up of their family. This was specifically brought to my attention quite vividly though my involvement with the Fresh Start Seminars.

Fresh Start Seminars began as a program for separated and divorced adults; to help them grow beyond their pain, to a point of acceptance in an entirely new lifestyle. The leadership team soon learned that one cannot effectively address the needs of the separated and divorced without helping them with their children. Many of the "single again" listed as their first concern the emotional survival of their children. Yet as I listened to their stories, I became aware that many well educated adults seemed to be doing it all wrong when it came the needs of their children. I am writing this book in hopes of reaching as many of these parents as possible.

The statistics for children of divorce are discouraging. Yet I believe that early intervention can make an enormous difference. Timely information and support for both children and parents, can lessen the negative effects of divorce.

In 1982, at the outset of the Fresh Start divorce recovery program, parents by the dozen asked me; "When are you going to do something for our children?" Their greatest concern was for their kids. I could hear their emotional cry for help, yet I felt ill-prepared to do anything. I remember thinking that someone should sponsor a program for these children. As I observed, listened and read the research on the effects of divorce on children, the burden began to touch me more and more.

Having worked in the Philadelphia School District for six years as a school psychologist, I was very aware of the needs of divorced kids. About 80% of the students referred to me for emotional or educational problems came from single parent families. To address this need within the school system, I started some small group counseling sessions specifically designed for the children of divorce. Through these few groups, I discovered just how necessary it was for these students to learn that there were other kids who where faced with similar difficulties; those who were dealing with insecurity, emotional pain, and the embarrassment of coming from a family where dad wasn't around or mom just didn't care. The opportunity to talk about their experiences and to encourage one another proved to be very therapeutic for them, and provided me with early insights into the needs of such children. In retrospect, I can see how I was being prepared for a ministry to children of divorce that would grow far beyond the Philadelphia area.

My next attempt to offer a program for children of divorce was during the Sunday School hour at the church where I was attending. I felt that the church was the ideal place for such a program because: 1) it typically addresses the needs of the traditional family at the exclusion of others, 2) the church includes the potential for whole family participation, and 3) the church should be a place of hope and healing, particularly to those who are struggling with difficult life issues.

The first week the class met with only eight students. It was difficult for them to come because they felt embarrassed, and like they were the only ones who did not fit into the "Christian family" stereotype. Some had no father at home. Others had a mother who had abandoned the family. Somehow it did not seem "spiritual" to admit to such problems at home. Eventually, the students began to open up and trust one another. They became a significant support group, and were a tremendous encouragement to me and to each other.

This class for the young victims of divorce grew in number, and as it did the students began to talk about other kids within their community that had no safe place to talk openly about what they were experiencing. They asked, "Why don't we do something for these children of divorce?". This was the very question their parents had been asking me for years. The students pointed to the divorce recovery seminar offered by Fresh Start for adults, and wondered why they couldn't have a similar seminar for kids. At this point all the pieces began to come together. So in 1987 we sponsored the first "Kids in The Middle" seminar at the Church of the Saviour, in Wayne, Pennsylvania. Over fifty children attended.

Today, Fresh Start Seminars and Kids in the Middle Seminars are held in many locations throughout the United States and two foreign countries. We attempt to conduct the weekend seminars simultaneously so that whole families can come together for a time of insight and healing. Brochures and other materials are available through the Fresh Start office at, 751 North Wayne Ave. Wayne, Pa. 19087.

This book is a direct outgrowth of that first

seminar, and the others that followed. It is designed to provide single parents and other concerned individuals with helpful suggestions and new insights to help children who are experiencing the break up of their families. With support and guidance, you can make a difference in the lives of these children—the truly innocent victims of divorce.

SECTION I

UNDERSTANDING YOUR CHILD

Chapter 1

Through the Eyes of a Child

I will never forget Eddie Hyser. I was in fourth grade in a typical suburban classroom. It seemed as though each of the girls had long blonde locks of hair. Each of the boys had straight brown bangs hanging over their eyes. We all waited anxiously for lunch, or recess, . . . or summer! It must have been a simpler time because I don't ever remember hearing about child abuse, child pornography, or even custody battles. Each child came from the typical American home with two parents, a stationwagon, and a safe neighborhood to play in. That is . . . except for Eddie.

Eddie was different. We all knew that Eddie came from a broken home. Whenever there was a problem in class, whenever something went wrong, or whenever there was a fight in the playground, we could rest assured that somehow Eddie was involved. We liked Eddie well enough but it seemed like one by one each of us would get in trouble when we played with Eddie. So one by one we either drew away from him or were forbidden by our parents to play with him.

I remember the time I got in trouble playing with Eddie and a couple of other boys. Someone was fooling with matches and somehow a fire got started. A fire burned a small field and the back of a garage. The police came and of course Eddie received primary blame. I got into trouble as well, but what I remember most was being told that I shouldn't play with Eddie. He was a "bad influence".

I don't know what happened to Eddie. I know that he was different from the rest of us. He acted differently and came from a different kind of home than the rest of us. You see, Eddie came from a broken home.

It seems funny to look back on that experience and realize that Eddie was the only classmate I can remember who came from a single parent family. Now I know that statistically there must have been many more families like Eddie's (just like I know there must have been child abuse, family violence, and custody battles). Yet I was completely unaware of their existence. It wasn't until I became an adult that I began to realize the extent of the problem that children have as a result of their family breakup.

I know that my childhood was a different day and age. Divorce statistics were much lower and for those who were going through divorce there was a much greater need to keep silent because of society's stigma upon them. Today, however, the problem of divorce is much more prevalent. Yet what many people don't realize is that in the mind of a child, the stigma and trauma of divorce are as real as ever.

Recent estimates tell us that one million children go through the experience of a family breakup each year. Just under one half of all marriages will end in divorce. And about 40% of all American children will spend some time in a single parent family before they reach the age of eighteen. Growing up in a divorced home is not a rare occurrence, but rather, a norm for today's society.

Today we no longer call these families "broken homes". The negative connotation and implied failure is too obvious within such a term. Instead we call them single parent families. However, the emotional effects are still the same.

As prevalent as divorce may become, in the eyes of a child (and in the eyes of the adult going through the divorce) they still feel as if they are the only ones going through such trauma. Why do they feel this way? Well, there are several reasons.

First, most people, and especially children, don't think about the problem of divorce until it affects them directly.

Secondly, children tend to be very ego-centric, which means they only pay attention to things that effect them. They tend to be selfish, only dealing with life's circumstances as they impact their own lives. Therefore, if they are not faced with the problem of divorce or family difficulties, they give it little or no thought.

The third reason children feel like they are the only ones going through such difficulties is because most kids (and people in general) tend to keep to themselves the emotional hurts and trauma of a family break up. Whether society causes it or not, people still feel the stigma of failure attached to the divorce experience, and therefore, do not talk about what they are going through. Most children are taught to keep family matters private. Therefore, they do not talk in school about what's going on at home.

While working in the school system, I was surprised to see how many students kept significant secrets from their classmates and teachers. Their elaborate schemes would include lying about weekend trips they had supposedly made with their "fantasy family", and making up wild stories about why both of their parents had not been able to attend a parent-teacher conference. However, their protection of the truth only thwarted opportunities that might have been available to them; such as support groups within the school, or even for a classmate to step forward and empathize with their experience.

An Overview

This book is divided into three sections. Section I which is called "Understanding Your Child" (Chapters 1&2) is designed to help you understand how children of divorce are different from adults who are going through divorce. The focus of the second section, entitled "Your Child's Reaction," (Chapters 3–7) is to examine how children of divorce are different from children from intact families. This will be done in a way which explores both short term and long term reactions to the divorce experience. Section III which is called "Helping Your Child" (Chapters 8–10) will provide specific guidelines as to how you can minimize the differences between your children and children from intact families, and help your children recover into a new and healthy lifestyle.

The Appendix at the end of the book is designed to provide you with a list of additional resources, dealing with specific issues. Whenever I address an issue which can be supplemented with other reading materials, I will insert "see Appendix". You can then find one or more recommended books on that topic at the end of this book. Hopefully, you will find this to be a valuable resource.

There are times when the information given might be difficult to hear, yet my desire is to emphasize that there is hope. I wish that each of you could meet some of the children and teenagers that I interviewed in preparation for this book. Some had recently experienced their parental break-up, while others had been in single parent or blended families for years. What I found in them I will not forget. They are some of the most loving, responsible and sensitive kids I have ever met. It is easier to overlook all of the negative statistics when you can sit down and talk with one of these students face to face.

As many of you read this book, you will feel great frustration with the suggestions that you know are beyond your ability to implement; or perhaps it is now too late to do them. Parents can literally torment themselves over circumstances that are completely out of their control. If you are to survive as a single parent you need to adopt the attitude which I believe is best expressed in the Serenity Prayer, which has been popularized by the Alcoholics Anonymous program.

"God, grant me the serenity to accept the things that I cannot change; the courage to change the things that I can; and the wisdom to know the difference."

As you read this book you must keep this prayer in mind. There are changes that you can make which will have a very positive impact upon your children. There are other circumstances, which might be quite negative, but unfortunately, you have no ability to control. It is these things that you must let go of, except as a matter of prayer. The really difficult part, and that which requires the greatest wisdom, is knowing which things you need to change, and which you should leave with God.

Perhaps a simple example would be most helpful. A common problem for divorcing parents, yet an important factor, is the parents attitude toward their children and toward each other. You *can* control you own attitude, but you can't control the other parent. Many parents expend a lot of energy trying to get the other parent to be more loving or responsible when the kids are with him or her. Yet this may only worsen the problem since your ex usually resents your input, while at the same time, you are only frustrating yourself. The frustration toward your ex can't help but be reflected onto your kids who now view you as too busy with your own problems to be accessible to them.

The alternative, and more helpful solution

is to pray for the other parent's relationship with their children, while you concentrate on loving your children as best you can. Concrete expressions such as hugs, listening to them, companionship at sporting events or concerts, etc. are obvious expressions of support that many single parents overlook because they are too busy thinking about what the other parent should be doing differently, or perhaps how they wish *they* were supported.

Understanding Your Child

In this first section of the book, which includes chapters one and two, I have sought to show how your child's reaction to divorce is different than your own. When we try to understand why children act and react the way they do in response to divorce we must first understand the different ways adults and children think. Many people mistakenly think of children as miniature adults. The truth of the matter is that children think and act very differently than ourselves. To effectively help children of divorce we must take these differences seriously and seek to understand how they effect our child's reaction.

Many parents believe that they need only to love and nurture their children, and that everything will turn out okay. As important as these ingredients are, it is impossible to truly love and nurture someone you don't understand. It takes a special effort to see the divorce situation through "the eyes of a child." This is emphasized by Dr. Stuart Berger in his book *Divorce Without Victims* (p.16):

> It is absolutely essential for the parent to realize that until the child reaches young adulthood, his view of the world and the people around him is very different from the adult's. Even the teenager who appears full grown in so many ways, is somewhat at the mercy of his continuing physical and emotional development. Your behavior toward your child, whatever his age, during the period of parental separation and divorce, must take into account his particular stage of development."

There are a number of important concepts for adults to understand about how children think if they are to help them through the trauma of divorce. In the next chapter we will look at a few of these key concepts. We will examine the ways in which the mind of the child differs from the mind of the adult.

CHAPTER SUMMARY

In this first chapter we have taken a look back and seen how attitudes toward divorce and children of divorce have changed. Yet there is still evidence of a significant stigma, perhaps one that the participants place upon themselves, when families break-up. Children who experience the divorce of their parents tend to feel very alone and different; different than other children and different than their parents. We have outlined how these differences will be covered within the first two sections of the book. Helping your child overcome these differences, and the negative emotions that go with them will be the topic of the third section.

Chapter 2

Why Don't We Think Alike?

If asked, "Why don't our kids think the way we do?", many of us would respond that it is because we are older and wiser than our children. While this is probably true, this explanation doesn't do justice to the complex developmental differences between the child and the adult. In this chapter we will take a closer look at some of the key differences. These include the difference between the concrete thinking of the child, and the abstract reasoning of the adult; the egocentric thinking of the child, and the adult's awareness of others; the magical thinking of the child, and the adult's sense of reality.

Concrete Thinking

At the age of seven, Kathy's parents were separated. When she spoke to me in counseling, she revealed that her father left the home because he and her mother had a fight. In reality, Dad was involved with another woman, and was planning a divorce so that he could marry his new lover. To Kathy, her parents had merely had a disagreement and would eventually make up. She went on to explain how she had had squabbles with her best friend, but that they always worked things out after a period of not speaking to each other.

Kathy continued by explaining that she knew her father was going to move back to their home real soon, because he had said that he still loved her very much. "Everyone knows that you don't leave someone you love," reasoned Kathy. "Both of my parents have always taught me that".

For Kathy, what she concluded was a combination of what she had been told and what she had experienced first hand. To a child this is their reality and this is an example of concrete thinking. As adults we have the ability to think abstractly. This is our ability to go beyond the specific situation and to make conclusions that we have not been taught. For example, if Kathy were older (perhaps 12 or older depending on her developmental maturity) she may have concluded that even when people love each other they don't always act in loving ways. Or she may have figured out that people don't break off their marriages because of a fight, and that there must be more going on than dad is admitting.

Another example of a child's concrete thinking is found in the way they view morality. Children usually begin to view right and wrong according to whatever their parents teach them. They can't reason for themselves yet. Later in life they begin to modify their parent's views according to their own experiences and input from teachers and friends. This "new morality", however, is merely a "black and white" view of what is right and wrong, based on the child's experiences. There is a general inability to deal with any "gray" areas, and therefore, children tend to be very legalistic.

As the child matures, so does their ability to reason abstractly. They begin to understand the intentions and motives of others. They become more flexible and understanding toward individual differences. Therefore they gain the ability to empathize with others even though they have never been through similar situations. Let me illustrate this development through some examples.

Why don't you steal? Your earliest memory as a child probably dictated that you shouldn't steal because your mommy or daddy said that it was bad. Perhaps later you observed other kids stealing toys and getting away with it. But just before you concluded that it was okay to steal, you saw someone get caught. So you learned that you shouldn't steal because you would be punished if you got caught. Hopefully, by the time you reach adulthood you begin to realize many other reasons for not stealing, even if you know there is no way you would get caught.

It is interesting to note that some adults never reach this final stage of reasoning. They go through life believing that it's okay to steal as long as you don't get caught. This is not only tragic, but it also indicates an immature or dysfunctional development of their moral reasoning.

In terms of the divorce experience, Kathy would be a good example. At age six, when her father first announced that he was leaving, she couldn't believe it because she always heard from him that he loved her and would never leave. At age seven when he actually moved out, Kathy was convinced that Dad left because of a fight, since that was what was going on while he was packing his bags.

In the absence of any other information, Kathy continued to believe this for several years. She thought her mom was good because she stayed at home, and dad was bad because he left. As she saw dad with another woman, she was jealous of his attention, but did not think much of it. That is until she was about ten or so. Then she began to make the inference that dad may have left *because* of this other woman. Now she was really angry at both dad and this new woman, who was now her step-mother.

As a teenager, Kathy did not support her dad's actions, but began to be more sympathetic and understanding toward him because she concluded, "Relationships are very complicated and I'm sure my dad had his reasons for doing what he did." "I know he didn't *want* to hurt us the way he did."

Concrete thinking deals entirely with the here and now. It is generally not concerned with consequences or intentions, nor does it take into account the feelings of others. Therefore, divorce is viewed in terms of how it effects me.

"My family broke up because of me." "I'm the only one going through this." "What am I going to do now?" I have heard these same phrases from the children of divorce again and again. Many children will not understand that there are other kids going through the same trauma, until they see them and talk to them personally. (Thus the importance of children's support groups.)

There is a transitional period somewhere between the years of 12 and 20 where teens gradually develop abstract reasoning skills. Divorce tends to delay this maturation process since children will usually retreat to a more comfortable, earlier learned stage of response, when they feel threatened. This is known as "regression."

I remember Peter. He first came to see me as a ten year old fifth grade student who was showing signs of emotional difficulties. His teacher referred him to me because he was very withdrawn and seemingly depressed. After hearing this description, I remembered how surprised I was when, after the first few minutes of our meeting, Peter began to open up and pour out his emotional concerns. He described his parents' separation which occurred when he was about five years old. He had many questions about it then, but didn't know how to ask them. He didn't remember any explanation as to why his daddy left.

For five years Peter lived with many unanswered questions. Since explanation and counsel had not been given, he concluded that he must have been pretty bad to have his father leave. Teachers and fellow students had no idea what was wrong because Peter never talked about it. He had become emotionally isolated.

Peter explained to me that he felt different because he was the only one in the school who had no father at home. His emotional isolation is evident in this belief because he was a boy in an inner city school with over fifty percent of its school population coming from single parent families! Still, Peter had no idea that these other kids were struggling through the painful breakup of their homes.

Peter's recovery was fairly rapid once we got to the heart of the problem and began to address the issues. I asked Peter to go home and ask his mom why she and his dad had broken up. In the meantime I called his mother and advised her to answer his questions as openly and honestly as she could, giving concrete examples as to why the marriage could not work. She was surprised by my request since this had happened five years earlier and in her mind it was all over and done with. What was settled in her adult mind was far from settled in her son's.

I then started a counseling group in Peter's class for those who were from single parent families. They openly shared their embarrassment of feeling all alone and different, yet by their presence, provided concrete evidence of the fact that others close by were sharing the same experience.

Before long, Peter began to feel more a part of his class. He no longer felt different or unusual. He began to speak up and interact with his classmates. He also learned from his mom that he was not to blame for his dad's leaving, and therefore, began to feel better about himself.

Divorcing parents should never assume that their kids will figure out what went

wrong. They will need very concrete explanations. This is one reason many kids have an
especially difficult time accepting separation
or divorce when there was little or no fighting
in front of them. I'm not suggesting that couples should *try* to fight in front of their children, but when there has been little concrete
evidence of a problem it is no wonder the kids
have a hard time accepting the marital break
up. Children need explanations and concrete
examples that they will be able to understand.

A child will generally relate the family
breakup to whatever disruptive event happened most recently in the home. This is another example of concrete thinking. The
younger the child, the greater the tendency to
react in this way, since their memories are not
as well developed.

When Sally, a seven year old second grader,
brought home a bad report card, her parents
yelled at her. This led to a big fight between
mom and dad, which culminated in her father's storming out of the home. It was not
surprising then that Sally informed me that
her father left and eventually divorced mom
because *she* had gotten bad grades.

Or the six year old boy who informed me
that his father left because mommy made the
wrong thing for dinner. You can imagine what
happened in that home just before daddy
walked out the door.

These are not isolated examples. Research

indicates that more than half of all children and teens who experience the breakup of their families believe that they were at least partially to blame. This phenomenon is due, I believe, to a combination of two factors—concrete thinking and "egocentrism", which will be covered in the next section.

As a parent, what can be done about my child's concrete thinking? Well, you cannot hurry a child's emotional or mental development. Like physical maturation, emotional development is generally predetermined and will only happen as a result of natural processes. However, divorce does tend to cause children to retreat in their development. This is not because their maturity process is slower, but only because insecure kids will tend to do and think things that are familiar and comfortable to them. They are not willing to stretch themselves with new challenges when their world is falling apart.

Fortunately, the developmental process balances out as children's lives begin to stabilize. As a parent, you need to try to provide as stable an environment as you can, as quickly as you can after the break up of the family. Stability, not finding another spouse, should be your number one priority.

Help your child by giving honest, clear information. Your child's questions deserve concrete answers. These are the only kind of answers your child will understand. "Why did daddy leave?" deserves "Because when daddy and mommy are together they fight a lot and that makes us both very unhappy." Or, "Because daddy loves someone else and wants to be with her." Or maybe, "I'm sorry but I just don't know why daddy left." If that's the truth, then that's what your answer should be. If you do tell your child you don't know why daddy or mommy left, you'd better discover an answer as soon as possible, and then let your child know the truth.

Egocentric Thinking

Kids are basically selfish. Most people are aware of that fact. However, did you know that it is a normal and necessary stage of development for all children to be "egocentric"? This means that children go through a time when they believe that the whole world revolves around them. For example, very young children believe that the entire family eats at 5:30 P.M. because *they're* hungry. Children are not capable of thinking any other way. And the younger the child the more egocentric they are likely to be.

When my daughter was one year old, she believed the only reason that mommy and daddy existed was to satisfy her every desire. She wined when she wanted to eat and again when she was tired. If you try to tell a one or two year old: "I'm sorry I can't pick you up right now but I'm busy," it probably won't get you very far.

Children retain some degree of egocentric thinking well into adolescence. They gradually change because of their increasing awareness of others and their growing ability to abstractly understand other people's point of view.

Let me share an example of how one's ability to think abstractly begins to change their egocentricity. Did you ever wonder why elementary and junior high kids can be so cruel to their classmates, particularly to those who are different or handicapped in some way? This is an example of egocentric *and* concrete thinking. "It doesn't hurt *me*." Or, "I don't care how it makes *them* feel." Children are generally unable to abstractly put themselves into another persons shoes and empathize with how they must feel. Therefore, parents should not expect their children to empathize with them over their divorce. The child can feel only their own pain.

As a parent you try to explain over and over why picking on others is wrong, or try to have your children understand a different point of view. Yet it seems like you're wasting your breathe. Then gradually, and strangely independent of your efforts your children enter high school and begin to feel empathy or compassion for others who are suffering. (Usually girls are about six months to a year ahead of the boys.) The teasing of the less fortunate dissipates to a point where many young adults will begin to really reach out to others less fortunate than themselves.

It is unfortunate but true that many teenagers and some adults continue to be thoroughly self centered well beyond the age where they should know better. This is usually not a reflection of their inability to understand how others feel (Unless they are developmentally or mentally retarded). Rather, it is more a reflection of bad habits, a family pattern, or a personality trait. The difference between the adult and child is that the child is not capable of adult thinking and relating.

How does egocentric thinking relate to the divorce experience? Divorce tends to make this egocentric thinking become more pronounced and obvious. Even the most giving adults will retreat emotionally, and immediately think only of self protection when they go through a divorce. Likewise children think only in terms of how all of this is going to affect them.

One teenager told me, "Here I am just getting to the point where I'm ready to start dating and my mom and dad pull this. How am I ever going to bring someone home to meet my parents when they're not even to-gether?"

Another student said, "Now that this has happened, what are we going to do about my birthday party next year?"

If you have experienced marital disruption, you may not remember hearing your child say anything like this. However, I can assure you that they have at least had such thoughts.

Egocentric thinking may cause children and teenagers to become angry with the custodial parent. They expect their parent to do something about the separation or divorce. And they may be too self centered to realize that their parent is powerless to change the circumstances. That is why a young mother who has been abandoned by her husband, can still be blamed by her children for "making daddy go away". Egocentric thinking in children of divorce can produce painful situations, but parents should remember that this is the child's nature, not a malicious behavior.

Another by-product of egocentric thinking is that children begin to greatly overestimate their own importance. Therefore, they cannot imagine anything happening that they did not somehow cause. This presents one more reason why so many children of divorce believe they were somehow to blame for their parents breakup. In the mind of the child, if everything revolves around me, then it is logical to assume that mom or dad left *because* of me.

For this reason it is extremely important that you constantly reassure your children that they had nothing to do with the break-up of the family. *Don't assume that they know this. Don't assume that they will ask if they have any questions.* Continue to reassure them as they grow and develop that they were not the cause of the break-up. They need to hear this over and over until they are mature enough to truly comprehend what they have been through.

You may ask yourself, "Why should I bother to explain such complex matters to my children if they do not have the capacity to understand such things?" The answer is because someday they will.

Each night, as I put my daughter to bed, I tell her that I love her. Does a two year old know what that means? Does she understand the meaning of love?

Your child hears the information over and over and gains a superficial understanding of what it means. As they get older, the depth of the meaning of your words becomes increasingly clear, until one day your children finally realize the significance of what you have been telling them all along.

So it is with children's understanding of the issues surrounding their parents divorce. Each new stage of development brings with it not only new understandings, but new questions which previously had not been considered.

Magical Thinking

As children, we always enjoyed a good nursery rhyme or a short children's tale. One reason we enjoyed them is because the characters always lived "happily ever after". This "happily ever after" thinking corresponds to our childhood magical thinking. Children believe that somehow everything is going to turn out okay because they wish it to be.

I recall the freckle-faced six year old boy in my office who told me that he felt bad because he wished his father were dead. I asked him why that made him feel bad. He responded that by wishing his father were dead, he was afraid that his dad would really die.

At the time I thought it unusual for this boy to believe that he could wish his father to death. Yet in terms of magical thinking it makes perfect sense. By thinking it, the boy believed he could bring it to pass.

Quoting from Dr. Stuart Berger:[1]

Magical thinking is a result in a sense of the child's perception that he is all powerful, that he causes all things to happen. Such thinking can lead not only to feelings of omnipotence, but to guilt and distress on the child's part. An understanding of magical thinking will help you to comprehend your child's sometimes puzzling reactions to divorce.

It is this magical thinking that causes most children of divorce to continue believing that their parents will eventually get back together, even after years of separation. I have observed this phenomenon numerous times, and research has born out the fact that most kids hang on to an unrealistic fantasy that their parents will someday be reunited.

Magical thinking is most pronounced in children between the ages of 4–8. The combination of egocentric thinking and magical thinking leads to the inescapable conclusion that, "my parents will get back together because that's what *I* want".

Billy was only seven, but was very mature because of what he had experienced. By the age of four he had witnessed his mother being beaten on a number of occasions. One time he had even called the police, and subsequently watched his father taken away in handcuffs. Even though his parents had been separated off and on over the past three years, he was surprised when his father left for the last time.

When Billy came to talk with me, he demonstrated a great deal of anger and resentment toward his father. In great detail he recalled incident after incident in which his abusive father had either hurt someone or broken something. Yet when Billy talked about the future it always included his dad moving home and interacting with the family in a healthy manner.

Was this merely a childhood fantasy or did Billy really believe that his miracle was going to happen? Young children have a hard time separating fact and fantasy. And adults have a hard time knowing what a child is thinking. Certainly for the child younger than six, there is a real belief that "mommy will remarry daddy and we will live happily together". After all, they believe that Santa and the Easter Bunny are coming as well.

After the age of six, children gradually begin to understand "make believe" and fantasy. However, many still believe that if they wish for something hard enough they can probably make it happen. This is a supposition that is supported by many of our favorite children's fairytales.

As they develop and become less ego-centric, children learn that they can't control adults nor make things happen by shear will. They cannot make Tinkerbell live again by wishing real hard. Yet some children of divorce continue to hold on to the hopeless fantasy that their parents will reunite well into their teenage years.

Patty was fourteen when she first came to see me for counseling. Her parents had been divorced since she was five. When she was younger, Patty used to see her father every other weekend. However, when she was eight her father remarried and moved about fifty miles away. From that time on, she saw her father only during major holidays, and for two weeks in the summer. As is usually the case, Patty did not like her step-mother, whom she always referred to as her "step-monster".

This is how Patty described her magical thinking:

> When I was younger I always dreamed about the day when my mom and dad would get back together and we could be a family again. Then when my dad got married to that witch, I felt like she had taken him away from us. Whenever I went over for a visit, I have to admit that I was kind of a brat. I sort of wanted my step-monster to be miserable, so that she would leave and then my mom and dad could get back together again. Now I realize that that will probably never happen. In fact, my mom told me that she and dad wouldn't get married again even if he and my step-mom got a divorce. Still, there are a lot of days that I think I wouldn't have had so many problems if only my parents had stuck together.

Even divorced adults can retain some aspects of magical thinking. They live with the expectation that their ex-spouse will come back, repent of all their wrong doing, and beg to be taken back. Or some may live for the day that "Mr. or Ms. Right" will come along and rescue them from a lonely life.

Is this just wishful thinking? Perhaps. But there is just enough little kid in all of us to keep our hopes alive. We need to be careful that we face our fantasies for what they are. Otherwise we will be left even more disillusioned, lonely, and despairing. (See Appendix re: Remarriage.)

CHAPTER SUMMARY

In this chapter we have examined some of the differences between a child's thinking and that of an adult's. In particular we have explored the ways in which concrete thinking, egocentric thinking, and magical thinking combine to cause the child of divorce to feel all alone, to focus on *their* heartache only, to blame themselves for some aspect of the break-up, and to hold on to the belief that someday their parents will get back together.

In the next section we will begin to look at the reactions of children who are experiencing the break-up of their parents. Now that we better understand the way our children think, we will be able to view their reactions "through the eyes of a child".

1. Berger, *Divorce Without Victims*, p.21.

SECTION II

YOUR CHILD'S REACTION

Chapter 3

Typical Reactions

Bobby was sound asleep when his mother shook him to get him up. "Get up, Bobby! Grab your blankie and teddy bear. We're going 'bye 'bye."

Bobby, who was only five and a half years old, quickly grabbed his things as his mother whisked him away in the middle of the night. He remembered very little beyond that point, as he drifted in and out of sleep. His mother took him downstairs, loaded him into a car full of family belongings, and drove off to Bobby's grandmother's house at the other end of town.

As Bobby woke up the following morning, and saw that he was at his grandmother's, he realized that he hadn't been dreaming about the night before. He was glad to be at his grandmom's, but was a little confused as to why they left so abruptly.

Bobby asked his mother all kinds of questions as they sat around the breakfast table.

"Where is Daddy? What are we going to do today? And when are we going home?"

His mother's evasiveness and tendency to change the subject, only caused Bobby to be more confused and curious.

Later that same day as Bobby was being put to bed in his grandmother's spare room, he once again asked his mother, "Where's Daddy?" and "When are we going home?"

His mother looked down at the ground and said, "I don't know where Daddy is, and I don't know when we're going home."

Bobby, who was pretty smart for his age, was now very confused. He knew that there was something wrong. Mom was acting funny. Grandmom and Grandpop were acting differently, and this wasn't like the typical visit to Grandmom's house. Daddy wasn't with them.

He soon began to wonder, "Did I do something wrong? I wonder if Dad is mad at me?"

"Well," he reasoned, "At least I haven't been yelled at or punished, so maybe everything will be back to normal tomorrow."

The days came and went with some days seeming almost normal. But most days Bobby wondered, "What is going on with my family, and why isn't Daddy around?"

The more he asked questions, the more his grandparents and his mother seemed to avoid giving answers.

Then one day, after more days than Bobby could count (several months), his mother came to him and said, "Bobby, sit down. We need to talk." Mom began to explain that she and Daddy were not going to live together any more. She talked about their fighting, about them not being in love any more, but Bobby didn't understand any of that. He only remembered that his mother said that he and his daddy were not going to live together. Oh, he liked his grandparents alright. And he liked living there with his mother, but he didn't understand why he, Mom and Dad couldn't live together again in their old house.

He had lots of questions, but didn't know how to ask. So Bobby only nodded his head, and ran off to play. He was still a little confused as to what was going to happen to him.

His mother, on the other hand, thought that things had gone really well. She avoided saying anything to Bobby up until that point because she didn't want to hurt him. Besides, for a long time she wasn't sure whether her separation from her husband was going to be permanent.

Now, after almost three months at Grandmom's house, Bobby's mom had come to the decision that she was going to seek a divorce. She had talked to her parents and had sought counsel from a pastor at the church. She finally concluded that she could no longer live a lie. The hardest part for her was telling Bobby. But once she made up her mind, she knew it had to be done.

When Bobby didn't object, cry or show any traumatic reaction to this difficult news, Bobby's mom assumed that he had taken it fairly well. She had no idea what was going on inside the mind of her child.

As the months progressed, Bobby's mother became more and more preoccupied with her own problems. She had re-established contact with her husband, most of which was unpleasant. They were discussing lawyers, finances, custody arrangements and settlements, which all brought about increased stress. One bright spot, however, was the observation that Bobby seemed to be fine. He had found a few friends in his new neighborhood, and seemed perfectly content with the new living arrangement.

Therefore, Bobby's needs and his adjustment became secondary to questions such as: "Where are we going to live? How can I support a household as a single parent? Will I ever be happy again?" She consoled herself with the thought that, "At least Bobby is doing okay."

That consolation didn't last very long. Bobby's mother had just worked through an arrangement where Bobby could visit his dad on alternating weekends, when things began to change.

Bobby was excited when his mom first told him about the visit to his dad's. However, within hours after that, he began to behave differently. At first Bobby acted very short and cold toward his mom. She just thought, "Well, he must have a lot on his mind." But soon, this distance turned more and more into overt anger that was displayed as temper tantrums, talking back and refusing to carry out even the simplest responsibility. To make matters even worse, it seemed as though each time Bobby returned from a visit with his father, he demonstrated even more anger toward his mom.

In school, Bobby was moving along in first grade. However, as visitation with his dad progressed, his grades began to slip. At a subsequent parent/teacher conference Bobby's mother was surprised to learn that her son was showing signs of anger in school. He was fighting in the schoolyard, picking on other kids, and displaying a general bad attitude toward schoolwork.

For Bobby's mom, this was the last straw. She decided to send him to the school guidance counselor so that she could gain some new insights into Bobby's problem. She assumed that his problems had something to do with his father, since she hadn't had any trouble with him before the weekend visits began.

A few months went by, along with several visits to the counselor. Bobby began to show slow, general improvement in his behavior. His temper tantrums lessened, and the school reported fewer problems. His grades, however, were still low. He was described as being very distracted.

Bobby's counselor reported that he was opening up in the sessions and sharing his concerns over his parents break-up. The counselor indicated that the visits to dad were not the cause of his problems, but that his insecurity over seeing his father merely triggered a reaction.

A year after the break-up of Bobby's family, he was showing fewer and fewer signs of anger, but now seemed more sad and withdrawn. His mother noticed him crying alone in bed a few times. He also seemed very distant and withdrawn whenever his weekend visits were approaching. She assumed that Bobby would work through these problems. After all, he was in counseling, and she had her own concerns to work through.

Bobby's school work remained poor, but at least he was passing. His teachers now described him as being somewhat withdrawn and uninvolved in general classroom activities. Most effected was his reading level and handwriting skills which seemed to regress as they approached the end of his first grade school year.

As time passed, Bobby showed improvement, but would revert to his withdrawn or sullen behaviors around the time of holidays, or any kind of special event within the family. He seemed very sensitive to change and was quick to display anger or sorrow.

This emotional roller coaster did not begin to level off until about three years after the separation of Bobby's parents. They were now divorced and there was a consistent visitation arrangement that seemed to be working well. Bobby's mom and dad were even talking to each other more civilly now. The only change in this slow and steady growth of improvement was when Bobby's mother went out on her first date.

Bobby, who was now eight, acted horribly that whole week. And when the person came over to pick up his mom, Bobby was at his all time worst. He acted rudely and refused to even speak to the gentleman. Throughout the following week, Bobby seemed very angry and rude toward his mother. It wasn't until weeks later that Bobby finally came to his mom and asked, "When are you and dad going to get back together?" His mother used this opportunity to explain once again to Bobby the finality of their divorce and to reassure him of their commitment to his well-being.

Today, Bobby is in high school (although he's now called Bob). He has the same insecurities and struggles that most teenagers experience. It's difficult for his mother to determine out how many of his problems are due to the broken home, and how many are part of normal teenage development.

Bob has a fairly good relationship with his mom, (as well as can be expected for a teenager), but rarely sees his dad due to their typically busy schedules. Bob's grades are back to normal, and he is fairly involved in typical high school activities. The only remnants of his parents' divorce seem to be those nagging questions that he still struggles with, but rarely talks about. These questions include:

- I wonder if my parents will ever get back together again?
- I wonder if I did something to cause my parents to get their divorce?
- Does my dad really love me, and if he does, why doesn't he visit very often? Is he really too busy?
- Why couldn't mom stick with dad just for my sake?
- I wonder what kind of parent and husband I will be, considering the fact that I've never really lived in a "normal" family.

Even though most of these questions have been answered, Bob still has them, nagging in the back of his mind, creating insecurity and a general hesitancy to trust in relationships.

Three Major Categories

Bobby's example might seem like an isolated case, yet it is fairly typical of those who work through their parents' divorce in a healthy way. A number of studies have demonstrated that children have similar patterns in reacting to their parents' divorce.[1] These reactions can be divided into three general categories.

The first category, which includes approximately one third (about 27%) of the children of divorce, contains those children who come through their parents' breakup in a fairly healthy manner, as in the case of Bobby. They go through the normal grieving process, experiencing denial, anger, depression but usually within two years, reach a point of acceptance. This acceptance seems contingent upon their parents' ability to work through an amicable settlement. This usually includes a reduced number of disruptions following the divorce, such as remarriage, a major change in lifestyle, or inconsistent visitation.

Typically, there are points of disruption beyond the two year adjustment period, such as when mom or dad might start dating, or maybe even get remarried. Yet this one third of the children of divorce demonstrate a fairly healthy adjustment. In fact, two years after the divorce, this group cannot be distinguished from other children whose parents have remained together.

A counselor, or someone very close to a child in this group might recognize the fact that many of them still have persistent questions about their parents divorce, even five to fifteen years later. Yet to an outside observer, they seem like a typical child with the same activities, values and concerns.

The second third of the children of divorce (approximately 34%) go through the typical stages of grieving, but seem to take a lot longer to go through each of the stages. In particular, they don't reach a point of acceptance within a two year time period, but rather tend to take anywhere from three to ten years. Generally there are more boys than girls in this category since boys tend to react more strongly and take longer to recover.

This middle group also tends to include children who have more family stresses to deal with than just their parents' divorce. These complications can include, but are not limited to:

- a major move, or major change in lifestyle (usually drastic decrease in financial status).
- remarriage of one of the spouses and/or the blending of families.

- alcoholism, drug abuse, or any type of physical abuse from either parent.
- a particularly "messy divorce," such as a prolonged legal battle or custody fight.

This middle category can also include children of divorce who experience "delayed reactions" to their parents' breakup. These children may seem fine for the first two years after their parents' separation, with little or no noticeable reactions. Yet three to five years later, with the onset of a new developmental stage (such as becoming a teenager), these kids will have a more severe reaction—testing limits, questioning authority, and generally distinguishing themselves as "troubled youth."

The long term effects, which last into adulthood, are much less noticeable for this group of children whose parents go through divorce. They finally do make appropriate adjustments, and have a fairly normal adult life. They do, however, show some evidence of difficulty with relationships, trust, and struggle with personal insecurities. This can affect their self-image, their friendships, marriages, and the way they raise their own children. Yet the research is inconclusive on these points since it is hard to determine whether or not there is a cause and effect relationship. In other words, we don't know how much of these long term implications are the result of

the parents' divorce, and how much would
have happened anyway because of the child's
personality, their genetic make-up, or other
life stresses that influence the child's development.

The final one third of children whose parents divorce (approximately 43%) are those
who never seem to recover from the traumatic effects of their family breakup. Their
anger, depression and general inability to accept their parents' divorce continues well into
their adult lives. This can result in school
failure, chronic unemployment, sometimes
early marriages, other times an unwillingness
to ever get married or have a family, an inability to trust others or to establish long
term relationships; and in the most extreme
cases, a higher frequency of drug or alcohol
abuse, personality disorders, and perhaps even
criminal behaviors.

Mike would be a good example of the child
who could not adjust. Mike was 27 years old
when I first met him at one of our church's
social functions. He was friendly, but somewhat hesitant in anything other than superficial conversation. As I tried to get to know
Mike over a period of several weeks, little by
little, he was able to peel away the veneer and
to expose more of his real self. As he did, a
much different person began to emerge.

I eventually recognized that Mike had a

drinking problem. Not when he was with me, or anyone from the church for that matter. He had a whole other set of friends with whom he would get drunk, and then usually get into some type of trouble. The trouble started with rowdiness and belligerence, but all too many times, evolved into fights, breaking windows, and eventual arrest.

I remember the first time I learned that he had spent the night in jail. I felt badly for him, but asked, "What's going on? How could you pick a fight with a cop?"

Mike's response was one that I later heard over and over again, each time he got into some trouble. "Well, when I was six years old my parents got a divorce. My dad took off with his secretary, and I didn't see him for three years." Mike would go on to explain how upsetting his childhood was, and how unfair it all seemed.

I remember saying, "Yeah, but Mike, that was 20 years ago. Isn't it time to move on with your life?"

Mike's response to my insensitive comment was filled with anger. "You don't understand! Nobody understands what it's like. Each time I get into a fight, or take a swing at a cop, I'm getting back at my dad. . . . I'd like to kill him for what he did to me and my mom."

That comment pretty well summed up Mike's excuse each time he was thrown in jail or sent to a drug and alcohol rehab center. Although I continued to reach out to Mike, he began to shut me out more and more, following the pattern of all of his relationships.

I eventually lost touch with Mike for several years. Then I ran into him one morning in a coffee shop not too long ago. He had the same innocent, boyish grin, and once again seemed very standoffish at first. I asked him about how he was doing, and where he'd been for the past several years.

Mike proceeded to tell me that he had just gotten out of prison for a drunk driving conviction.

Surprised by this I asked, "How did that happen?"

Mike, who was now over 30, recited a now familiar response, "Well, when I was six years old my parents got a divorce. . . ."

It would seem that Mike will never fully recover from his parents' divorce. His story, while probably more severe than most, is similar in its long term effects to almost one third of the children of divorce.

Would Mike have had problems with drinking and self control if his parents had never divorced? Probably—no one can really know for sure. It would seem, however, that the inclination was always there, and that the divorce was only a catalyst for the problems. No one knows what other catalyst might have set off a similar reaction; or if *any* catalyst would have triggered such an intense response.

CHAPTER SUMMARY

In this chapter we have divided divorce re-actions into three general groups. These groupings are based on research which finds that approximately one third of the children of divorce show little or no reaction to their parents break-up. Yes, they do go through their own grieving, but if you were a teacher in a typical classroom, these kids would ap-pear to be no different than your average stu-dent.

The second third are those children who seem to have a more severe reaction, but eventually (3–10 years later, depending on the age of the child) work through their grieving, and go on to live productive, healthy lives. Once again, if you were a teacher, you would notice a difference in these children, in their behaviors, emotions, or even schoolwork; but if you visited with them five years later, you would see them as "well adjusted".

The final third, are those children who have severe reactions and never seem to recover from their parents divorce. Our jails and reha-bilitation centers house a very high percent-age of "adult children of divorce" with some estimates as high as 85%. The good news, however, is that two thirds of the children of divorce work through their parents' divorce and achieve reasonably healthy adulthood.

For those with children of your own, one of your greatest desires is to see your children adjust as well as they can to the stresses of the family breakup—to be within that "first third" of the children of divorce. There are many things that parents can do to help their children adjust in a positive way. Later in this book we will explore some of the things you can do to help your children. But first, we will cover the feelings your child is likely to have as he or she initially adjusts to your divorce.

1. Joan Kelly, *Longer-Term Adjustment in Children of Divorce*, Journal of Family Psychology, December, 1988.

Chapter 4

The Initial Stages

"My summer days couldn't have been more perfect. The iridescent sun was a perfect match with the Caribbean blue sky. I would be on the green grass in my bare feet, looking up at the clear sky and think to myself how lucky I was to have all this, and to love the world I was living in.

At least I loved it until the night came. That's when it would start. The kids were supposed to be sleeping soundly and unaware of the whole nightly ordeal. But, with me being the oldest, I heard the same thing every night. The yelling and screaming, the slamming of doors and chairs, and the cry of frustration and anger. Dad would get mad and Mom would run away crying in frustration. I didn't know what to think. Was it me? Or my brother or sister? Were we causing all this trouble? I didn't understand, it was all so confusing.

I would pray for progress or some kind of

change in the situation, but I must not have prayed hard enough, because it did not change. Then came the night of real terror. There was a knock at my bedroom door, so I called, 'Come in.' In walked my mom and dad, brother and sister. My first thought was that I had obviously done something very wrong, and so I said, 'Whatever it was, I didn't do it.' But instead of laughing, there was only total quiet. My dad was the one who finally broke the silence. He told us that he had something very serious to talk to us about, and we should all listen closely. My brother, sister and I sat frozen on the edge of the bed as my mom and dad explained to us the horrid situation. When they were done, we knew of the problems we would have to face, and the changes we must undergo in this new thing called divorce. My dad was the one who left the next day for an apartment. It was arranged that we would see him on the weekends.

From that day on, whenever I went outside, no longer was the sun as bright, or the sky as blue. Now, reality had darkened the world around me, and I had to learn to cope and live with the consequences of divorce".

—a fourteen year old girl.

The initial time period, just beyond your announcement to the kids that your marriage is over, is a very critical time. In any crisis, what happens immediately after the "blow up" is very significant. For many of you, this is in the past and it is already too late to undo some things that should not have been said or done. For others, the way this is handled is beyond your control because your former partner refuses to cooperate. Whatever the situation, the "beginning of the end" is for many the most difficult time.

Being awaken in the middle of the night by your parent's fighting; abruptly leaving your home and father on the eve of a special holiday; having to call the police while you watch your father beating your mother; and feeling like your whole world is falling apart as you suddenly move to another town without your mother's knowledge, are all situations which I have heard described by children of divorce. It is an extremely emotional time for all parties involved, and as a parent, you want it to go as smoothly as possible for your children.

Since you are most certainly going through your own grieving process, (Read *Through The Whirlwind*, by Bob Burns for help in working through your own grieving—see Appendix.) you may be in no condition to recognize or address the emotional needs of your children. You may not even think about their emotional needs until months later. By that time there is the chance that some initial damage has already been done. Therefore, this is a very critical time period for you to seek help from others- family, friends, a school counselor, or some other type of professional. If your family or friends are as emotionally wrapped up in the problem as your are, then they may not be the best source of help.

It is also important for you to know what you can expect from your children. That is, in terms of their reaction, you need to know what is normal and what emotional stages they will experience as time progresses.

It's just like when your child gets the flu. You can see that they don't feel well and you know they have a temperature. You become concerned, however, because you don't know how serious it is and whether or not your child will get worse. So you take them to the doctor. Upon examination, your doctor tells you, "Yes, they have the flu. There's a lot of this going around right now. Just have your child get lots of fluids and rest. They'll feel better in a few days."

You go home feeling much more relaxed, even though nothing has really changed. Your child is still sick and the doctor has really done nothing to help you. So why do you feel better? Because 1) you found out that their symptoms were normal, 2) that other kids are going through the same thing, and 3) that they will get over it, just give it some time.

So it is with your child's reaction to divorce. I want to describe to you what are the normal symptoms, assure you that there are other kids going through the same thing, and reassure you that they will reach a point of acceptance, even though it may take more time than you thought.

The amount of time that it takes for your children to recover from the trauma of your divorce, and the intensity of their reaction may vary, but the emotional stages that they go through seem to be fairly consistent. Researchers have indicated that a child's reaction to divorce approximates the same stages of grieving that adults experience when they lose a loved one through death or the breaking off of a significant relationship. This seems to be true across a wide range of ages, including adult children of divorce.

From preschoolers to adult children, there appears to be an instinctive process of grieving. Yet the way the stages of grieving are experienced, and the speed of the process seem to be dependant on a number of factors, including but not limited to: the age of the child, the sex of the child, the way the child relates to both father and mother, the way mom and dad relate to each other, and the stability of the child's environment.

The Initial Phase

For the sake of simplicity, I have arbitrarily divided the grieving process into three phases: the Initial Phase, the Secondary Phase, and the Acceptance Phase. Within the Initial Phase, which is the topic of this chapter, there are several predominant emotions which are typically handled by two basic reactions—*denial* and *anger*.

These two reactions, and the behaviors that go with them, are the first two stages of the grieving process. In essence, this is merely the child's way of handling their emotional crisis. Most children will jump from stage to stage, often regressing numerous times before reaching a point of acceptance. Even when acceptance is the predominant condition (usually 2—5 years after the marital disruption), children will relapse into grieving whenever new stresses enter their lives, extending well into their adult years. These "residual" influences can effect their own marriages, as well as the way they raise their children.

Figure #1 illustrates the way children deal with input during the "Initial Phase". The arrows represent input from the environment, which is just a fancy way of saying "all the junk your child gets hit with on a daily basis". The outer circle is the defense system, which is a natural and instinctive protection of your "inner self". The inner self is just an expression that I use to describe the essence of your personality, or your true self.

As indicated by the diagram, during the initial onslaught of information regarding the break-up of the family, your child protects him/herself from this devastating news by deflecting the information. At first they use denial. But as shown in the illustration, as much as your child denies the truth, some information still seeps in, so that you are eventually forced to "face the music" (represented by the fading doted lines). At that point, many children become very angry, and therefore, will use their anger to deflect what they can't deal with.

Sammy, at age five, did just that. When his dad first told him that he was going to be moving out, Sammy acted as if nothing had changed. His dad was elated that the dreaded news was so easily received. But as Sammy's dad unpacked items into his new apartment, he found red magic marker scribbled all over

PHASE ONE: INITIAL REACTIONS

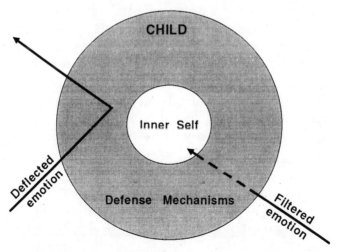

Defense Mechanisms – Denial and Anger

several of his dress shirts. When he confronted Sammy with what he had done,
Sammy threw a temper tantrum, kicking and
screaming at his dad.

When I say that your child *uses* denial or
anger as a defense mechanism, this is not
intended to imply intentionality. Defense
mechanisms are largely unconscious. In other
words, your child does not say "now I'm going
to use my anger to keep from getting hurt".
Rather these emotional responses are like a
"blinking eye" reaction. When the eye is
threatened by an object, it blinks automatically in order to protect the eye surface. So it
is with the child's (and our own) defense
mechanisms. They "kick in" automatically
when there is a threat of emotional hurt.

Let me further clarify that even though
someone is in the Initial Phase, that does not
mean that they won't feel a full range of emotions, including: rejection, guilt, confusion,
fear, sadness, anxiety, etc. However, this phase
is distinguished by the fact that your child
will primarily deal with all of these feelings
through denial and anger. Now we will discuss the nature of denial and anger in children
of divorce within a variety of age groups.

Denial

Denial corresponds with the initial realization that, "My parents are getting a divorce!"

For some children this is an insight or conclusion that they reach on their own due to
overwhelming evidence of a problem. For
others, their first indication of a problem at
home is when mom or dad sits them down
and tells them the disturbing news. For most,
however, it is a combination of evidence
within the family and comments that have
been made to them by both mom and dad.

Whatever the case, children are not prepared to handle the news that their whole
world is about to come apart. This initial
shock is met with comments or thoughts
such as, "This can't be happening to me." Or,
"I'm sure they will work everything out; I
know my parents really love each other". As
seen in Figure #1, both of these comments
serve to deflect the truth.

Denial is similar to an actual "physical
shock". When people go into shock they are
literally able to temporarily numb the pain.
They might even show a greater level of ability; as when an injured accident victim is able
to rescue his entire family from a burning
vehicle. It isn't until later that the pain becomes acute, and the person realizes the extent of their injuries.

So it is with the child who first learns that
his or her parents are about to separate or
divorce. The mind goes into a type of emotional shock which temporarily numbs the
pain. I believe that this is a God given, natural

reaction, that we as parents should recognize and accept, and maybe even be thankful for. Denial of an emotional blow has its place in preparing the way for eventual acceptance.

Preschoolers

As in the example of Billy, (from Chapter 3) his mom was pleasantly surprised at how well her son seemed to take the news of his parents divorce. This is particularly true of preschoolers (ages 2–6) who are not at a developmental stage where they can understand the implications of their family breakup. Their concrete and magical thinking (remember from Chapter 1?) tell them that "mom and dad have had fights before. I'm sure they'll work this one out too". Many times they work through their denial through "fantasy play", in which they can pretend that everything works out just fine, and that "we all live happily ever after".

Denial spares the preschooler unbearable pain. You see, to a preschooler, their whole world is their family. They have no sense of, "well at least I still have my friends, or my job, or my church activities", as we adults usually have. For them, their whole world is about to fall apart. How can we expect them to understand and accept?

Don't be surprised if your preschooler does not express any of these emotions. They typically cannot express what they are thinking or feeling because they usually don't even know themselves. You have to try to understand their feelings by watching their behaviors' and then trying to interpret what's going on inside their mind.

One interesting reaction was recently shared with me by the mother of a preschool boy. After telling her young son the devastating news of his father's imminent departure, her son responded with, "Can I go out and play now?"

The comment might be considered unusual, but the underlying reaction is typical. Many parents report that their children seem go to on as if nothing has changed. The only noticeable difference might be that the children are a little more "clingy", especially whenever you might want to go out without them.

School Aged Children

For the school aged child (ages 6–12) you can expect a similar type of denial, however, you might hear more questions about how their life might change. At this age your children are just as stunned, but now they have a better intellectual ability to reason and question.

Now don't quote me on this one, but in some cases (including some teenagers) your children's behavior might even *improve* during this time. One parent told me that her two children suddenly stopped bickering with one another. They started doing their chores without being told, and were generally very well behaved. "How do you explain that behavior?" she asked.

The explanation which I gave has to do with this "denial stage". You see, as the child denies their own feelings, they may also recognize the fact that mom or dad is really hurting, and therefore, they "cool it" around the house for a while until "things blow over".

Now unfortunately, this reaction doesn't last very long. As the denial wears off, the child becomes aware of their own hurts and begins to act out their own pain. Enjoy it while it lasts!

Teenagers

For the teenager, denial can take the same forms as those already mentioned, but may also demonstrate itself through increased activity outside the home. This, by the way, is the way in which many adults handle their denial. By immersing themselves into work or a hobby, or by just refusing to think about what is going on.

Teenagers typically are seeking independence no matter what the family dynamics are like. So when you add the news that "your mom and dad are splitting up", then you'll see many teenagers begin to seek excuses to get out of the house. Whether it's a ballteam, a church youth group, or a new intense friendship, your teenager may seem to vanish in order to avoid or block out the pain he or she may be trying to deny.

One mother of a sixteen year old boy recently told me about her son's relationship with his girlfriend.

"My son had been dating this girl for about six months. Once I told him about his father and I breaking up, he seemed to lean on her completely. I'm glad he has her, but I'm concerned that he's over at her house *all* the time! He eats there, hangs out there, and seems to do everything but sleep there. He was never like that before his father left. Do you think it's because he's mad at me?"

It is more likely that the boy is in the stage of denial. Her son has merely intensified his relationship in order to take his mind off (or deflect) the problems he has to face at home. This can work for a while, but sooner or later her son will have to face the reality of his parents' break up.

Adults

For those who are considered to be adults (over 18), there is the expectation that they will not be affected as much by their parents break up. Research has not found this to be true. In the initial phase, adult children of divorce tend to react much like their parental counterparts. Their denial merely reflects their disbelief that this could be happening to them.

Many times this age group is away from home, and therefore, less dependant on mom and dad. Yet they still seem to go through the same denial that younger children experience. Their way of dealing with the denial is usually to immerse themselves into their work, school projects, or other social relationships. Another common tactic is to pretend that the divorce will have no bearing on their lives.

One college student told me, "I'm on my own now. What happens to my parents at this point doesn't effect me. I'm more concerned for my little brother."

This same student later dropped out of school, partially due to grades, but also because things at home were "falling apart". Whatever the reason, the truth was that he *was* effected, and that this student had a lot to work through before he could go back to school again.

Then there are the adults who are married and have families of their own. When they hear about a parental divorce they tend to react with the same disbelief. They many times fall into the role of "parenting their parents" (as do some younger adults and teens), trying to mediate the conflict. Although this may be a natural reaction, parents should not encourage their adult child's nurturing instincts since this is an unhealthy family pattern. Instead, adult children of divorce need to care for themselves and their own families. Divorcing parents should assure their children that they will seek the help they need from a more neutral and appropriate person.

For adults, the denial does not last as long as in children. Since they possess higher order thought processes and abstract reasoning skills, they tend to become more quickly aware of what went wrong, who did what first, and why things are not going to work out. Their biggest dilemma is usually their loyalty conflicts, which remains the major issue throughout the rest of the grieving process.

Moving On

Is this denial bad or wrong? Not at all! It's a normal, God given reaction to devastating news. It's what keeps us from going crazy when the news is too difficult to comprehend. Without denial we would be overwhelmed by anxiety. We all use it as a defense mechanism. Children in particular will use denial since they have no other way of controlling adults or their actions.

How can I help my child move beyond their denial? The truth of the matter is that there is very little that you can do. And perhaps you shouldn't even try, since this is a natural defense for working through pain. Give your children time to adjust their thinking, and let it run its natural course. Try not to increase their anxiety by reacting in extreme ways.

Children, particularly the younger ones, are not sophisticated enough to figure out that by staying in denial they can avoid some of the bad feelings they have about the divorce. Actually we adults (and some teenagers) are more often guilty on that count. So it's not like they are using denial on purpose. They will move on in their healing when they are emotionally ready to deal with it. Creating a stable environment as quickly as possible will help the child pass through this stage more easily.

Parents can help their kids deal with the reality by giving them clear, honest answers to all their questions. Trying to gloss over the truth to save their feelings will only help them to avoid reality for a little longer, which needlessly extends the healing process.

A common example of how you can help your child face reality is one that you face every holiday season. Think about that dreaded "first Christmas" as a separated couple. Parents constantly explain to me how dad is going to come over Christmas Eve or

Christmas morning so that we can spent Christmas Day together just as we always have. Even though this noble effort seems to be in keeping with the spirit of peace and good cheer, I'm afraid it only increases the anxiety and feeds the denial of our children (and many times the parents).

It's not like you are actually lying to your kids, but in a way you are acting out a lie, assuming your marriage is really over. Acting happy and "together-like" helps your children hold on to the fantasy that "our family will be fine". Remember, the quicker you begin to build new traditions, such as: "We go to Dad's on Christmas Eve and spend Christmas Day with Mom", the sooner you and your kids will be able to move on with your lives—and heal.

Giving your children honest information and not play acting in front of them, will help them realize that the separation and imminent divorce of their parents is a reality that they will have to face. As they do, one of the first feelings that comes rushing in is insecurity and fear. And this should not surprise us. It's incredibly unsettling to find out that your whole world is falling apart.

Such is true even for those eager and sometimes overly-confident teenagers! They want to go out and discover a whole new life for themselves. One that is completely independent from their parents. But what they don't tell you, and may not realize themselves, is that they also want to come home to a "safe" environment. They become painfully aware of this need once that safe, familiar homelife is taken away from them. Now they become angry, because after all, "it's not fair!". For teenagers, "fairness" is judged in relation to their own needs.

As we have seen in Figure #1, even though we deny, some realizations inevitably trickle into our "inner selves". (As demonstrated by the doted lines.) Once these realizations accumulate to a point where we must face certain issues, we are filled with fear and anxiety. The way most children of divorce handle their fears and anxieties during the initial phase is with *anger*. This is considered by many to be the second stage of grieving, and is another way we all deflect painful information that we may not be ready to deal with. Anger, therefore, is just another tool that we and our children use to protect ourselves from the reality of the situation.

Anger

As time goes on, and more of the reality filters through your child's defense mechanisms, they begin the recognize that they cannot make the problem go away through denial. Their fear leads them to the very natural reaction of anger. Once again, as seen in the diagram, all they are doing is deflecting the pain of the situation elsewhere. Sometimes it is deflected toward a person. While other times it is deflected toward the situation in general. In either case, the child avoids dealing with reality by blaming others. The "Oh no, not me" of denial, evolves into the "Why me!" of anger.

One boy said, "It's like when you first hear about it you can't believe it's true! Then when you realize that it might actually happen, you get mad at your mom or dad or both. You think, how can they do this to me! It's not fair!"

This is probably one of the most recognizable and familiar stages. Whenever people think about children of divorce, one of the stereotypes that comes to mind is the child who is the terror of the class or neighborhood. The Eddie Hysers of this world. Even though this stereotype is overstated, it is certainly true that children of divorce typically carry around unresolved anger. The ways in which they deal with their anger depends a lot on their personality, their sex, and their age.

Sex Differences

In terms of sex differences, it is generally accepted that boys feel and demonstrate anger more openly than girls. This is not always true. Certainly personality differences can alter this generalization, but across most age groups, one can expect boys to react more angrily than their female counterparts. And even though they may get beyond the anger stage as their predominant reaction, they continue to show signs of anger throughout all of their stages of grieving, sometimes lasting a lifetime. This does not mean that girls do not get angry. Some show more anger than boys. But for the most part, girls are better able to express their feelings, and therefore, may be more adept at resolving their angry emotions.

Or, (to give equal time to another theory as to why this phenomenon occurs) our culture has taught girls how to internalize their anger, so that we see less evidence of an angry reaction.

One possible exception to this rule of thumb that boys react more strongly than girls, is found in several studies about adult children of divorce. When parents divorce with adult children in the house or out on their own, it is usually the girls who have a more severe reaction. Their anger may be more internalized, but nonetheless they seem to bear the brunt of the dissolving family.

Two possibilities as to why this occurs are: 1) Boys tend to move out and distance themselves emotionally, more quickly. 2) Girls tend to be more nurturing, and place more value on the family relationships. Therefore when things begin to fall apart, they feel more compelled to get involved, or upset about their inability to change the situation.

Age Differences

Age differences are a bit more complicated than sex differences, due to the diversity of developmental changes as outlined in Chapter Two. For the younger child (under 12), their anger is often misplaced. This means they don't always direct their anger toward an appropriate target.

These angry feelings are typically expressed toward one or both parents, but can also be directed toward siblings, the "third party" involved, and many times toward self. The younger the child the more likely they are to blame whoever happens to be around. This means that even though they might be angry at dad for leaving, they will take their angry feelings out on the custodial parent (mom).

For all the reasons outlined in Chapter Two, children under six years of age will many times blame themselves for their parents break-up, and therefore, will feel anger toward self or *guilt*. The younger the child the more prevalent the guilty feelings are likely to be. These children believe that all of the families activities revolve around them, and therefore can't help but feel like they must have done something wrong. This reaction can be par-

ticularly concerning to parents since it can
lead to depression, self condemnation, and in
the worst case, self destructive behaviors.

Guilt can be a predominant feeling for other
age groups during the angry stage, but as your
children get older they are better able to understand your explanations that "you had
nothing to do with your Daddy's decision to
leave". In fact, the research has demonstrated
that among children of divorce who are 18 or
older, the feelings of guilt over the parental
break up are almost non-existent.

Young Children: Preschool and Schoolage

How is anger displayed? For the youngest of
the children, aggressive play and temper tantrums are increased, particularly when you
(the custodial parent) want to go somewhere
without them. Or anger may be most evident
right before or after the days of their visitation with the noncustodial parent.

One parent recently told me about her
"well behaved" daughter who would turn into
a terror every other weekend, right about the
time of her father's visitation. The mother
asked me whether or not this was good
enough reason to try to cut off visitation
rights, since she was obviously reacting so
angrily to the thought of her father's visit.

I responded with the fact that this is a fairly

typical reaction to the insecurity and anxiety the child feels about the changing of households. This reaction will subside as the child works through the angry stage and becomes more accustomed to the fact that they visit with dad every other weekend. There may be absolutely nothing "scary" about visiting with dad. And usually the child is fine once they get there. Yet many have strong angry reactions just before the visit is to commence. I conclude that this is more a reflection of the anger they feel about the situation than anger toward a person.

This does not mean that there are not times that you might need to "look into" what's going on while your kids are at the other parent's house. Don't jump to premature conclusions just because your children are resistant about going over. It's probably best to seek a professional counselor's advice if visitations continue to be a problem for you and your kids.

Small children are also not as sophisticated at distinguishing who is to blame for the break-up. This may be particularly frustrating to the parent who wants to be sure the children know how innocent he or she was in the marital mess. Children will tend to blame the one who leaves, since their loyalty will be toward the one who "sticks with them", no matter what the circumstances might other-

wise dictate. Contrasting this point is the fact
that even though they may blame the parent
who left, they are more likely to vent their
anger onto the parent who is present. This is
not only because of availability, but also because they feel more free to show their anger
to the parent with whom they feel most *secure.*

This has been a common complaint that
has come to me from many a discouraged
single parent. One mom recently stated, "I
can't understand how my child can stand
there and shout, 'I hate you Mommy!', when
I'm the one who does everything for her while
her father does nothing!".

Try not to be overly hurt or upset by your
child's anger. Remember, they are probably
venting their anger over the situation, or may
even be using you as a sounding board because
they trust that you won't leave them like
their other parent did. One child put it this
way. "You've already seen your dad leave, and
even though you're mad at him, you want to
make sure he'll come back again next weekend. So you take it out on your mom because
you kind of know she'll always be there for
you."

This by no means dictates that you, as the
custodial parent have to put up with abuse
from your child. Try to understand their hurt,
and try not to over react out of your own
frustration over the situation; but feel free to

discipline the child who is behaving disrespectfully or who is verbally abusive. They may be testing you to see if you care enough about them to discipline them. Remember, your child may try almost anything to get your attention, even if the attention is negative. Better to get mom's attention through acting out than not to get her attention at all.

Teenagers and Adults

For the teenager, displays of anger are certainly not foreign. In fact, many parents express the following dilemma: "I can't figure out how much of my teenager's anger is due to our divorce and how much is just typical teenage rebellion". Nevertheless, when divorce occurs, many teens show increased signs of anger, resentment, and rebellion.

Unlike their younger siblings, the teenager will try to assess blame, and then may target their anger toward a particular person. This is why you may see the teenager refuse to visit or even speak to one of their parents. If the target of their anger happens to be the custodial parent (usually mom), then the rebellion and sabotage within the home can become so unbearable that mom may give up and allow her teen to "run free" or just send the teenager to live with dad.

When the lines of blame are not so distinct, which is much of the time, the teenager's anger may be more generalized. This can be evident in their attitude and behaviors toward parents and siblings, teachers and school, the church and God, and at times, their friends and themselves.

Teenage boys tend to be more aggressive with their anger, while both boys and girls can demonstrate their anger through more passive means- called "passive aggression". This can be seen in many teens through their lack of cooperation, moodiness, and ability to create general turmoil for those around them. A good example of passive aggressive thinking was expressed by one teen who said, "I don't get mad, I just get even!".

Ginny was just such a teen. She was fourteen when her father moved out. Within a matter of months, what was once a fairly compliant child, was now growing more and more resistant. She started by defying and talking back to both parents. This carried over to some rudeness at school which prompted a phone call from the school counselor. Next to be affected was her attendance at church. She began to resist getting up on Sundays, which evolved into a refusal to go. Her involvement within the church youth group faded, and was replaced with a new set of friends who were described as "questionable" by her mother. All of these changes only seemed to alienate Ginny from family and former friends.

In counseling, Ginny revealed a great deal of anger. Yet the target of that anger did not seem to stay focused. Her "generalized" anger meant that she blamed everyone else for her confusion and growing isolation. This became almost self destructive as Ginny was now only associating with those who would lead her into more trouble. Indirectly Ginny felt like she was getting back at those who had wronged her, but in fact she was mostly hurting herself. The child who is trying to "get even" can never "get ahead".

"It's not fair !" is a common theme of the teenager who is angry about their parents divorce. In many ways they are right. It isn't fair. Anger is just a natural reaction to this injustice. The real question is—"How will your child display their anger?". As a parent, you cannot keep your child from experiencing this anguish, but you can try to help them work through their anger. Acknowledge that their sense of fairness *has* been violated, but explain also that life isn't always fair. Hopefully, this experience will become an object lesson that the child will use throughout their life.

Guilty feelings during this stage are much less likely for the teenager than for those who are younger. They are usually too busy blaming everyone else for their problems to feel guilt about something they might have done. In a few cases, however, the teenage child of

divorce may feel guilt over their parents
break-up, particularly in situations where
they have been the focus of difficulties or
arguments in the home.

For the adult child of divorce, there is little
evidence that they feel any guilt at all, but as
previously stated, there may be an increased
feeling of responsibility to help, particularly
among the women. They may try to get involved, and are much more likely to feel anger
toward the active agent in the divorce (the one
who is seeking the divorce). Depending on the
maturity of the individual, the anger of an
adult is usually better managed than with
teens or younger kids. Adult children are able
to articulate their concerns, and therefore,
have a better chance at resolving their angry
feelings. If they don't live at home, they don't
have to deal with the constant tension and are
more likely to have a relationship with both
parents.

Helping Your Child

How can I help my child work through
their anger or guilt? Acknowledge your child's
anger, and if it's appropriate, affirm their right
to be angry. This allows for more of the reality
of the situation to actually filter into your
child's life, as illustrated in the diagram. This
can be very healthy!

Encourage the free expression of their feelings. If you even suspect that they may be

blaming themselves at all, make sure you reassure them that the decision to end the marriage is strictly your's (and your spouse's), and
has nothing to do with their behaviors or actions. If your children are young, they may
not understand this the first time you tell
them, so continue to reassure them pe-
riodically just to make sure.

If you are the target of their angry feelings,
try not to be defensive. It is most important
that you are able to *listen* during this crucial
time. It would be quite natural for you to
defend yourself, or to even shout back at your
child. But remember, your child is reacting
out of feelings of fear and insecurity- a need to
be sure that they are loved. Their behaviors
might even be an unconscious test to see if
you will still love them even when they are
bad. By listening, you reassure your child that
you will not abandon them.

What if it is the absent parent who is the
target of my child's anger? Now we come to
the really hard part. Once again, you must sit
by and neutrally listen. *Do not join in and
bad-mouth your ex-spouse!* As much as you
might agree, or think your child would appreciate your reinforcement of his ideas, it's important that you resist this temptation. Oh
sure, your child might appreciate it for the
time being, but in the long run it will only
hurt your child's emotional growth and probably put them quickly into a position of de-
fending the other parent. It is very much like

the old adage: "*I* can criticize my family, but *you* had better not try it".

Michael's mother found herself in this dilemma. She reported, "Whenever Michael gets back from visiting with dad he seems extremely agitated. He complains about everything."

"Dad did this . . ., and dad did that . . ."

"You'd think he hated going to his father's. But when I agree with him and suggest he just not go anymore, he immediately jumps all over *me* and then starts telling me all the wonderful things that he likes about his father. He sure has me confused."

There are some times when helping your child deal with their anger requires you to go well beyond just listening to them or helping them to express their feelings. There are the temper tantrums, the long silences when they refuse to speak, and the belligerent behaviors which seem to push your buttons.

As difficult as it might be, try to ignore the minor infractions and outbursts. And when it is needed, don't be afraid to lovingly discipline your child. (See Appendix re: Discipline) But above all, try not to be drawn into a fight. To respond in kind will only increase your child's anger and make you feel as immature as your children are acting. Please note, however, that you will "blow it" from time to time. This is inevitable. After all, you are going though your own struggles. When you do mess up, tell your children you were wrong and then start over again, trying to model an appropriate way of dealing with anger.

In the worst of situations, your child's anger will lead them into behaviors which you cannot afford to ignore. Unfortunately, teens in particular have many dangerous options available to them at a time when they might not be thinking very clearly. Drugs and alcohol are the most obvious examples of this, but other problem areas include school truancy, promiscuous sex, and even criminal activity. If you suspect your child of participating in any such activities, seek professional help as soon as possible. You must take this type of behavior very seriously, and try to "nip it in the bud". By quickly treating the symptoms, you have a better chance at keeping the problem from getting worse, and you have a greater opportunity to get to the heart of the problem before your child becomes unreachable.

Professional help can come in the form of a counselor or psychologist, especially if you know of one who specializes in treating children of divorce. If you are not familiar with anyone like this, check with your family physician, the school psychologist, or a pastor who knows your situation and can made an educated referral.

Moving On

As in the case of denial, eventually enough

truth filters through the defense barriers that our children once again get a glimpse of reality. They realize, unconsciously, that their denial did not work, and that their anger only brought them more pain. Gradually they are able to process what is going on in their lives and what is happening to their family. And even though they are distorting the reality around them, they are now able to deal with it at some level. This is what indicates that they are moving on to the "Secondary Phase".

Denial and anger are presented here not as an exclusive list of the reactions your child will have when first confronted with separation or divorce. Certainly there are many emotions and many reactions. In addition, even though these phases are presented in an orderly, sequential fashion, your children may "jump" from one phase to another—over and over again. In other words, even though your child moves well beyond the initial phase, don't be surprised to see them regress back to some form of initial reaction whenever a new family trauma or change occurs. These type of regressions are occasionally evident during holidays or anniversary dates of the break-up; whenever you child is reminded of the depth of their loss.

How long does this Initial Phase last? The speed at which your child moves through the stages of grieving is a very individual process.

This depends on their personality, as well as how easily your divorce unfolds. Now I know that there is no such thing as an easy divorce, but it does help your recovery and the recovery of your children, when you and your ex can work together for an amicable separation and divorce. This will be discussed further in a later chapter.

In any case, you have to expect that it will take several months for your child to work through this initial period. It is not unusual for some children to take a year or more to work through their denial and anger. If you find that they seem to be stuck in one of these stages, you may want to seek professional advice. It is also noteworthy that some children experience "delayed reactions" , as discussed in Chapter Two. This delay can be a form of denial in which your child seems to have no reaction at all until a year or more later. Then they seem to just begin the grieving process. This is most likely in the case of the very young child (5 and under) who does not understand what has happened, or how it will effect their lives. As they grow and develop, they may start their grieving process one or more years later.

CHAPTER SUMMARY

In this chapter, we have examined your child's initial reactions to the news that a separation or divorce is about to occur. They are immediately flooded with a myriad of emotions, but generally react in two basic stages. The first is denial, which is the result of the child's inability to cope with the devastating news of the family break-up. Once your child gains a glimpse of the reality of their situation, they are filled with fears and insecurities about their lives and future. This fear pushes your child into the next stage which is anger. Anger about the situation or toward one or both parents.

These initial emotions can last anywhere from a few weeks to a few years, but a more normal time frame would be 2–10 months. Helping your child move along in the healing process involves your giving them honest, clear information, and encouraging the open expression of their emotions. As the truth filters through their defensive exteriors, your children will be able to move on to the next phase of the grieving process. Additional guidelines on helping your child move along in the emotional stages will be presented in the third section of this book.

Chapter 5

The Secondary Phase

"I know when my dad first left I was really mad at him. I blamed him for all of the problems in the house, especially when I would see my mom crying. That would make me want to go over to his place and punch him out. But when I was with my dad, I never said a word about how I was feeling. I was afraid he would leave for good. Then, as I started to accept the fact that my parents were getting a divorce, I think I just gave up. I gave up on school, the track team, and on just about everything. I didn't feel like doing things any more. I spent most of my time just sitting in my room, listening to my tapes."

—a fourteen year old boy.

Beyond the initial denial and anger stage, children usually become very frustrated, because they learn that they can't make the problems disappear by pretending they're not there, and because their anger only seems to make the problems worse. These realizations lead your child to begin feeling even worse than they did before. They are unable to protect themselves from all of the "junk" going on around them, or from the onslaught of negative feelings.

In terms of the diagram from Figure #1, even though your child has been able to deflect many of the incoming arrows, some painful realizations have managed to filter in and affect their inner selves (represented by the doted lines).

In addition, as time passes, your child becomes emotionally stronger, and therefore, better able to face the pain. Their defense mechanisms ease a bit since they are now better able to handle the reality of the situation. With more and more of "the truth" effecting your child, soon they can no longer use deflection to protect themselves. This change marks the beginning of the "Secondary Phase".

This new phase is distinguished by the fact your child's primary way of dealing with their situation has changed from deflection to distortion and filtering of information (see Figure #2). Now, the arrows of input are able to reach the inner self, which means they begin to effect the child. Perhaps even causing your child to feel worse. You will notice, however, that the input is distorted or faded by remaining defenses. These new defense mechanisms are necessary because even though the child

PHASE TWO: SECONDARY REACTIONS

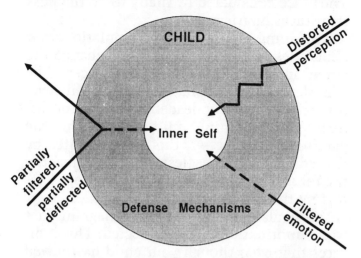

Defense Mechanisms – Bargaining and Depression

is stronger, they are still unable to honestly or fully deal with their changing world.

Your child's feelings during the Secondary Phase may be very similar to what they felt during the Initial Phase: rejection, anger, confusion, sadness, guilt, frustration, and depression. The difference is that now they are handling the feelings differently. Instead of denying their feelings, or deflecting them by blaming others, they are now allowing themselves to feel some of it. Not fully yet. They are still too fragile for that. But they *are* able to begin letting these feelings sink in.

What new methods does your child use during this phase in order to handle their emotions? Usually *bargaining* and *depression*.

These are considered by many to be the next two stages of grieving.

Bargaining is a form of manipulation your child uses to lessen the pain, or change the situation in order to make it more acceptable. And depression is a natural emotional reaction which actually deadens the pain, or distorts all incoming information. In the diagram on Figure #2, this is represented by the fading doted lines (lessening the impact of the information), and the zigzagged lines (distorting the information).

You'll also notice from the diagram that some information is still deflected. This indicates that even though your child has moved on to the Secondary Phase, sometimes information is still too hard to deal with, or the child regresses to the point that they once again deny or react in anger.

The great paradox in this phase is the fact that *even though your child is emotionally stronger, they are probably experiencing more pain*. This is just part of the grieving process. In many ways, your child must hurt worse, or "hit bottom", before they can begin to get better. This is called "bottoming out". We will see this more clearly as we now discuss both bargaining and depression in more detail.

Bargaining

Even though the "bargaining stage" is presented here as the third way your child may try to deal with their emotions, this defense mechanism may be observed throughout the Secondary Phase. It is probably one of the most difficult stages to understand and to recognize. Simply put, it is when your child becomes so frustrated with the situation that they try to find simple solutions to a very complex problem. The complex problem is the fact that their parents are getting a divorce. The simple solutions are the child's feeble attempts to manipulate their parents into a desired outcome.

Younger Children: Preschool and Schoolage

For young children the motivation behind bargaining is frustration. Your child merely wants to make the pain go away, and many times the goal is "to get my parents back together". For the younger child this usually involves fantasy and magical thinking; but for those who are eight or older, actual manipulation of the situation is very apparent.

It is hard to recognize the bargaining stage because there is some form of bargaining throughout all of the stages. In fact, as I describe its symptoms, many of you will think, "My kids do that all the time". Once again, what distinguishes this as an actual stage is the fact that your children will use bargaining as their *predominant* defense mechanism. This usually comes out of the frustration

that; "My anger, guilt, or sadness only make
me feel worse. The only way I'm going to feel
better is to get my parents back together." Or,
". . . is to see if I can help my mom find a new
daddy for us."

If these quotes don't sound at all familiar to
you, that's because your children do not verbalize these ideas, they only *think* them.
Since your younger children are not sophisticated enough (usually) to figure out how to
make their wishes come true, they only fan-
tasize about their parents getting remarried to
each other, and then sometimes will unconsciously act on those fantasies.

Ryan would be a very good example of this
phenomenon. Ryan's mom and dad had been
divorced for about three months. He had been
showing signs of anger toward mom and toward authority figures at school, but was now
finally settling down to more normal behaviors. It was at this same time that mom
began to date a man she met at night school.
Well, those of you who are single parents can
probably predict what happened next. Whenever mom's new friend came over to visit or to
pick her up for a date, Ryan behaved at his all
time worst.

Ryan, who is only seven, probably did not
think, "Now, let's see how I can sabotage this
relationship". In fact, while talking with me,
he said he liked his mother's boyfriend. But
what he doesn't say and may not even realize

is that this new man in his mom's life is a threat to his ongoing fantasy that someday mom and dad will get back together.

Another common example can be found in Tracy, who at age four knew that if she pushed her mom "to the limit" right around bedtime, mom would call dad to come over and discipline his daughter" Of course, as soon as dad arrived, Tracy would go right to bed with barely a whimper, which only encouraged mom to call dad the next time it happened. This went on a number of times until Tracy's parents realized that the motivation behind the misbehavior was to get mom and dad back together for the evening.

Teenagers and Adults

For the older child, especially your teenager, the attempts at manipulating the situation are usually much more overt. They may verbalize their desires, and then work behind the scenes when you don't comply with their wishes. I have heard many an example from children of divorce who talk about how they relay (or mis-relay) messages between their parents; changing the tone or content of the message in order to accomplish some purpose; usually trying to draw parents together, or drive them further apart. I find it incredible to see how often this works, and how long kids can get away with this type of bargaining. It seems to work best when parents do not speak, but use their kids to communicate to each other; literally putting them in the middle.

Other teens, who are perhaps less devious, will not give misinformation, but will give just enough detail, or omit just enough to convey the message they want heard. One fourteen year old girl did this as she told her mom how hurt dad seemed; how bleak his apartment looked; and how lonely he appeared. Perhaps if mom felt sorry for him, she would not be as mad.

For adult children of divorce, bargaining usually involves their getting into the middle of things. If not to mediate and get parents back together, then to comfort one or both parents through their suffering. This very difficult role takes its toll on your children. The effects of your divorce can sometimes be just as devastating to your adult children as it is for you. That is why they try to do whatever they can to help make the pain go away—just like you do.

Helping Your Child

The best way to thwart this type of activity is for parents to not allow their children to be "caught in the middle". By this I mean negotiate with your ex-spouse person to person. If you did not get your support check for that month, don't ask the kids to "just mention it to your father when you see him". The better you are at *co-parenting*, the more likely it will be that you will have open communication with your ex. And then your children will be less likely to believe that they can change their home circumstances through any form of bargaining.

Bargaining is a lot like denial in that the motivation behind both is to help make the pain go away. And for both stages your part is to help your children deal with the reality they will *have* to face. It seems cruel to say that you shouldn't "sugarcoat" the situation in order to save your children some pain, but the truth is that the sooner your children learn the truth, the quicker they can begin to deal with it and move forward in their lives.

One final note about the frustration and bargaining that children experience: These feelings may not present themselves as a separate stage but may instead be inter-mingled with other stages, including denial, anger, guilt, and our next stage to be discussed- depression.

Depression

We have described all of your child's emotional reactions, so far, as defense mechanisms. Yet it is hard to imagine depression as a defense against anything. Actually, their depression is a natural reaction to overwhelming life change and pain. It's like an

electrical switchboard which shuts down
when it is overloaded with current. This crisis situation may inconvenience a lot of people, but without such safeguards, there may
have been a fire or explosion.

Such depression is referred to as a "reactive
depression", since it is in reaction to specific
life stresses. This is different from a depression caused by a chemical imbalance, hor-
monal change, or hereditary predisposition.
These latter depressions need to be treated by
a qualified professional. (Contact your family
doctor for a referral if such a depression is
apparent.) Assuming your child's depression
is merely reactive, you need to understand
that this is a natural and necessary part of
your child's grieving. It is also the way your
child protects him/herself from more exten-
sive damage. So in this sense, depression is a
defense mechanism.

Most of us reading this section are familiar
with the depression and anxiety described in
this stage because at some time in our lives
we experienced it first hand. However, many
of us may be surprised to learn that children
get depressed and overly anxious too. I have
talked with four and five year olds who have
mentioned suicide as an escape from their
problems.

Depression usually begins once the reality
of the situation sets in. By this I mean that the
child has moved beyond denial and recognizes

that they *cannot* control their parents or the situation. Their anger and guilt has only made them feel worse, so they give up. They have learned that they are totally helpless to change the situation, and therefore, must accept the way things are. That's depressing !

Being in the depression stage does not mean that your children will not slip back into anger or bargaining. In fact it is common for people to slide back and forth between all of the stages like an emotional roller coaster, on a daily basis.

Most of us know how we feel when we're depressed or anxious, but how can you recognize it in your children, especially when they are too young or unable to express how they feel? Childhood depression is different than adult depression because it can be so varied. For example, children can show depression through sadness, increased anxiety, distractibility, resentment, sullenness, regression, confusion, lack of interest in social activities, loss of appetite, and even through acting out behaviors. The way your child demonstrates their depression will depend on their age and personality.

Younger Children: Preschool and Schoolage

For the younger child, (8 or under) depression can appear as sadness and withdrawal, while others (especially the boys) may actu-

ally show signs of increased activity and acting out. This has been called "masked
depression" because it seems almost opposite
of what we regard as typical depression. Even
though these children seem to have a high
activity level and to be quite anxious, the
underlying feeling is still depression. They
merely cover their sadness with tasks or trouble making.

If your children are in school, you can expect to see lowered school performance, due
to increased distractibility and regression.
This regression is an interesting phenomenon
where children seem to go *backward* developmentally. Toilet trained preschoolers will
start having "accidents" again; others will regress to "baby-talk", and skills that were once
known will seem to be forgotten.

I remember one incident while I was con-
sulting in an area elementary school. A
teacher came to me and said that she thought
one of her first grade students had a brain
tumor. I asked her why she thought that. She
replied, "Brian started the school year knowing how to write his name and all the letters
of the alphabet. As the year progressed, he
began to make mistakes on his last name,
then didn't know how to write several letters,
and now only seems to be able to write a few
letters. Is it possible for a child to forget that
much in just a few months?

My immediate response was, "What's going
on at home?"

As we looked into the situation, we found out that dad had left the home about two weeks into the school year, and that since then there had been a lot of discord in the home.

Regression seems logical when you view the sense of loss from a child's perspective. As they move along, growing in knowledge and independence, suddenly their whole world seems to start falling apart. They immediately begin to go back to an earlier, more comfortable stage of development. This helps them feel more secure. They stay there until they feel comfortable enough to "step out" again into new directions. As adults, don't we do the same kind of thing? We find ourselves retreating back to our parents house, or taking an easier job, or acting more like a teenager than an adult.

In addition to regression, some preschoolers and young children will demonstrate their depression through insecurity and an almost "clingy" dependance. Your child may seem overly anxious, complain of stomach aches, lose their appetite, lose sleep, or develop a "school phobia". The school phobia, and the way they cling to you whenever you try to go out, is really just a symptom of the insecurity and anxiety they feel. The insecurity that 1) "Will mom leave me too?" 2) "I wonder if dad will come back." 3) "How will we pay our bills?" 4) "Will we have to move, or will I have to go to a different school?" 5) "Why didn't

God stop this from happening to us?". These and a hundred other questions like them all enter your child's mind, with no apparent answers.

For the young child there is little for them to do but wait for the situation to become more stable and secure. This will take time. Time for them to grow up, and time for them to see that they can begin to trust again. As a parent, you want to provide an environment that will speed this healing process.

Teenagers and Adults

For the teenager and the young adult, depression is more recognizable because it is similar to the feelings of an adult. As your child matures, they gain in ability to express the way they are feeling. This assumes, however, that they are willing to talk to you. Usually, one of the by-products of the depression is the feeling that no one understands and no one cares. This alienation is particularly strong in teenagers. The divorce just acts as a catalyst for a more extreme rebellious reaction.

Other symptoms of depression include: eating and sleeping disturbances, a very low self image, expressions of worthlessness and hopelessness, regression to a more immature stage, lowered school performance along with heightened distractibility, social and peer difficulties, lack of interest in activities which were once of interest, and in the worst cases, escaping reality through drug and alcohol abuse.

Fortunately, these symptoms are the exception rather than the rule. Most pre-teens and teenagers seem to go on as usual, yet they have a sense of loss or sadness which is only noticeable to those who are closest to them. As a parent you may sense their increased isolation and sadness. It may seem more like a preoccupation and/or emotional distance.

This was the case for Jenny. She showed a very slight reaction throughout her parents separation and divorce. She didn't even react when her father remarried just a few months after her parents divorce. Her mother thought she was doing well, but referred her to me when she noticed that Jenny was losing interest in many of her former hobbies, and her school reported her to be falling behind in her work.

When Jenny first can in, she appeared to be a very mature fourteen year old. She talked about how well she was doing with all of the changes in her life, as if she were trying to convince me that she didn't need to be there. As we talked over a period of weeks, she began to talk about her loss. "I was always considered to be 'Daddy's girl'. I had no idea that he had a whole other life with some other family. Now he's married to Pam, who has her own two children".

"He comes around here to see me about

every other weekend. But what hurts the most is knowing that he is spending every night with Pam's kid's. I'm sure he'll start loving them more and more until he forgets all about me. My life will never be the same!"

You can probably see how Jenny's sense of loss is very similar to that of her mom's. Jenny feels like she has been betrayed and replaced. Yet when I asked Jenny why she had never talked to her mom about any of this, she said, "My mom feels bad enough. She cries a lot and I know she feels like she's been dumped. I need to be strong so that at least she won't worry about how I'm doing".

As previously mentioned, boys tend to have a more severe reaction. And so it is with depression. During this stage junior high and senior high aged boys can go through a year or more of distractibility, problems in school, social difficulties, and passive aggression. Just as with "masked depression" in the younger kids, these older students (boys in particular) can underhandedly try to get back at others as part of their depression.

Matthew, at age fifteen, was demonstrating this type of depression. He had gone through the denial and anger stages. Now, about a year later, he was beginning to settle down and let the reality of the situation sink in. As things at home were mellowing out, mom was beginning to think that the problems were through.

Therefore, she was quite surprised when she got a call from the school asking her to come in for a parent/teacher conference.

It seems Matthew had not been bringing in his homework assignments, including several large projects. In addition, he had been cited for being late to several classes, and had two unexcused absences. Needless to say, Matthew's mother was shocked at this revelation.

When she confronted Matthew with his behaviors, he merely shrugged his shoulders and grunted out non-responsive answers. Over a period of weeks, the situation showed no improvement, so his mother brought him in for counseling.

At first, Matthew was a very unwilling participant in the counseling sessions. But as rapport was built, he began to share his basic apathy about life, and in particular, toward his schoolwork. To quote his reasoning, Matthew said, "My parents obviously don't care about me. My dad's gone, and my mom is always either at work or out with her friends. My needs and concerns are not important to anyone, so why should I care about my schoolwork. Besides, the only time my parents talk to me is when I screw up. So this time I really screwed up! You should hear them screaming now".

It doesn't take a psychologist to figure out that Matthew is depressed and seeking attention. However, he is also mad at his parents and believes that he is indirectly getting back at them by doing poorly in school. He needs to learn how to appropriately express his feelings, and then recognize that his performance at school is only hurting himself. (We spent the next five weeks trying to get him to understand that concept.)

For the adult child of divorce it is sometimes surprising how depressing divorce can be. Many parents think that because the kids are older and maybe even out of the house, they won't be as effected. But, having talked with dozens of adult children, I know that their parents' divorce can literally send them into a tail spin. They have reported loss of appetite, loss of sleep, inability to focus attention, excessive daydreaming, lack of ambition, and a general feeling of numbness. When the adult children are still (or back) in the home, they sometimes end up feeding into their parents' pain by discussing the events over and over. One woman reported it this way, "We had a house full of depressed people, mirroring each other's anguish and suffering. This went on for months, until one of my sisters started coming out of it. As she got help for herself, she gave the rest of us the courage to begin looking forward".

Helping Your Child

In time, your children, whatever their age, really do "bottom out". They reach a point at which they give up. They stop trying to get mom and dad back together, they stop believing that life can go on without adjustments, and basically come to the point where they are ready to face the truth, no matter how hurtful it might be. Once they begin to deal honestly with their situation, they are on their way to a point of *acceptance.*

Even though the depression stage can be one of the longest and most uncomfortable stages, it does serve several very useful purposes. Let me list a few.

1. Since people usually "shut down" during times of depression, this stage tends provide your child with more peace of mind than the previous stages. (This reaction varies depending on your child's personality.)

2. They probably stop trying to control the situation, and begin to accept things as they are.

3. For the first time, they are beginning to deal honestly with themselves about the divorce, and are taking a serious look at how it will effect their lives.

4. The depression usually signals the fact that your children are at or near the bottom of the grieving process, and therefore, are bound to start "looking up" soon.

It is important to remember that this stage

is a very normal, and necessary part of the grieving process. As parents, we should not negate, nor rush our children's emotions. Don't say to your children, "Stop moping around. Your father's gone, and the sooner you get used to the idea, the better." Give them the time that they need to grieve. You don't want to add to their pain by reminding them about all they have lost, but you also don't want to force them to pretend that all is well, when they still hurt inside.

Here are a few other suggestions for helping your child through their depression:

1. Encourage them to talk to you about their feelings. Make sure you always acknowledge the depth of their loss.

2. Don't be afraid to grieve in front of them, but don't model to them a sense of hopelessness or hysteria. They need to learn from you that it is okay to cry, but they don't need to see you out of control.

3. Help your child accept the reality of the situation by telling them the truth. Don't hold out false hope in order to keep them from being hurt. As discussed before, it's better to answer their questions honestly so that they can begin the healing process earlier. Honesty will also help them as they try to rebuild new trust in you.

4. Try to find some healthy activities for your

child to get involved in. This could include a hobby, church activity, or school function which might help your child focus on something a little more positive.

Of course, if the depression persists, you will want to consult an appropriate professional. And if the despair or emotional mood swings seem severe, (such as suicidal thoughts) you need to seek immediate help.

How Long Will This Go On?

The Secondary Phase can take as much as a year to work through. And the entire grieving process can take two or more years. Once again there are wide individual differences in the amount of time it takes your children to reach a point of acceptance. These are considered to be the "short term" effects of divorce on children. The "longer term" effects are generally thought to be those which occur after the child reaches a point of acceptance, usually 2–5 years after the actual divorce. These effects will be discussed in Chapter Seven.

Why does the healing process take so long? Rather than a slow steady progression of emotional growth, the healing process can probably best be described as "two steps forward, one step back". As your child moves toward acceptance, maybe even reaching that point at times, inevitably something happens to send them right back down that emotional roller coaster that we call the "slippery slope". That is why your children will need to go through at least two full years before they become confident in their acceptance.

They need to experience at least two Christmases, two Easters and two birthdays in their "new family" before they can feel comfortable with their new living arrangement. And this assumes that the transition goes fairly smoothly. If you add on a new marriage by one of the parents, or a relocation, or any significant family change, then you can see how their recovery can take a much longer period of time.

CHAPTER SUMMARY

In this chapter, we have examined the Secondary Phase in your child's recovery from divorce. We have seen how your children move from denial and anger, through bargaining and depression, and eventually approach a point of acceptance. During this process, we have seen how the child many times will feel worse, even though they are progressing. This paradox continues until the child eventually "bottoms out". Barring any new disruptions, this is followed by a period of gradual movement toward acceptance.

In addition, we have discussed how you can

help your child move along in their recovery without pushing them before they are ready. As parents, you need to expect that this grieving process will take at least two years for your child to complete; and that any significant family trauma or change will lengthen the recovery. Providing your child with a warm and stable home environment, along with a consistent, stress-free visitation arrangement, are the best ways to help your child reach a point of acceptance.

Chapter 6

The Final Stage: Acceptance

"As bad as my parents divorce was, I know that it has made me the person I am today. I think I've gained a different way of looking at the world. It has forced me to take a more realistic view; that life doesn't have to be fair! I know that things will not always go the way I want them to. Therefore, moving on with my life has to be a process of accepting what has happened, and trying to make the most of it. In school, I don't see too many kids with that kind of attitude, so I figure, they haven't had to struggle with anything as difficult as I have."

—a seventeen year old boy.

Every parent wants their child to reach a point of acceptance as quickly as possible. What we must remember is that the grieving process is a natural reaction which must be allowed to run its course. We all have the tendency to believe we're a little further along than we actually are. And so it is with our children. We want to believe that everything is fine, but we are usually premature in our belief that the adjustments are now over. This was the case for the Logan family.

Mr. and Mrs. Logan had separated only months prior to my getting involved with their children. Mrs. Logan brought them to me for counseling early in the separation, not because there were significant problems, but because she wanted to head off some of the more serious difficulties. She hoped that as a family, they could recover as quickly as possible.

Indeed, the early intervention seemed to be a big help in that Mr. and Mrs. Logan were able to amicably resolve a custody and visitation agreement. For both of them, the chief concern was consistently the welfare of their three children. In joint sessions with the whole family, the children were informed of the arrangements and assured that they were loved by both parents.

This concerted effort paid off in that both parents and children were spared the depth of anger and fighting that most fractured families experience. The children in particular expressed only a little denial early on, and then went through a period of anger about their situation which I would categorize as mild.

Within a period of months, all three children seemed to be moving along nicely in their new lifestyle. There was very little resentment or depression, and in fact, the children were encouraging both mom and dad to "go out and find someone new". Mom spoke to me at that point about concluding their counseling since everything seemed to be going so well.

Unfortunately within a week of that conversation, things began to fall apart. It started with the oldest son Mike, who was about fourteen. The school contacted mom because they were concerned about Mike's "lack of effort in school, and increasing social withdrawal". Upon further investigation by the school psychologist, it was concluded that Mike was experiencing a significant depression and was in need of counseling.

One by one, the other two children began to experience a similar reaction. All three were back in counseling, but this time to talk about their feelings of loss and sadness. They felt little energy for anything as "trivial" as schoolwork, and now were very upset whenever mom went out, let alone trying to date. They seemed to need additional support and security at home; at a time when mom was making her own adjustments to a new job and new lifestyle.

We were all a little surprised at how long the feelings of sadness persisted. It seemed like every time things were finally moving along, some disappointment or disruption would set everyone back a bit. This "up and back again" growth toward acceptance lasted for a good year before the children truly began to get over their grieving.

Today, some two years later, the children have moved on with their lives. They are dealing honestly with the trauma of their parents divorce. This does not mean that there are not some difficult moments around the holidays, or that they don't get mad at mom or dad from time to time. (Sometimes it feels like all of the time.) These things happen in all families. But now the difference is that the children have the emotional energy to handle each new situation and to honestly face the implications it will have on their lives. This is called *acceptance*.

The reason I have shared this particular example with you is to point out that you need to count on at least a two year recovery time, even when the situation is amicable and parents provide a helpful support system. The amount of time for recovery is merely lengthened when parents refuse to cooperate, or otherwise continue the battle well after the divorce agreement is final.

The Defense Mechanisms

In terms of our diagram, as seen in Figure #3, the Acceptance Phase is distinguished by

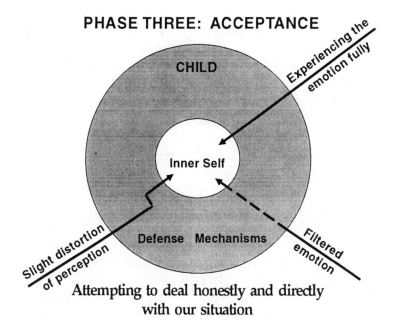

PHASE THREE: ACCEPTANCE

CHILD

Experiencing the emotion fully

Inner Self

Defense Mechanisms

Filtered emotion

Slight distortion of perception

Attempting to deal honestly and directly
with our situation

the fact that now your child's defence mechanisms are within the "normal range". Instead
of deflecting or distorting, they are now able
to allow new information about the family or
the environment to impact them directly.
Most information passes through the defensive layers, and is then able to reach the "inner self" without alteration. This is the way
healthy individuals deal with their world.
The defense system is still in place, however,
because we all need protection at times when
information is too hurtful to absorb. We continue to filter and distort some information
for the rest of our lives. Yet when in acceptance, we are able to deal honestly with most
input from our world; and then learn and

grow from the experience. This is known as coping!

How is this theoretical diagram practically played out in my child's life? Let's examine how the Acceptance Phase is experienced within specific age groups.

Preschoolers

In this age group I believe it is very unusual for a child to reach a point of acceptance. In actuality, most preschoolers merely delay their reactions until they reach a developmental stage in which they can understand what has happened to them and their family. You see, in order for these children to honestly deal with the consequences and ramifications of their parents divorce, they usually need to wait a few years before they are completely aware of how it will effect their lives. Once they understand that, and come to terms with this realization, then they have reached acceptance.

This is why many children who see their parents split up at such a young age will have a fairly mild reaction within the first couple of years. They may even appear to have no reaction at all. Then when they reach six or seven years of age, they may go through a modified grieving reaction. It's as if they just realized the extent of the problem. Then as they enter each new developmental transition, (school-age, teenage, adulthood) they may experience another reaction due to new realizations of the effects of the divorce.

For example, a child of two might show little reaction at first. Then after a period of insecurity and/or anger, they seem to be fine with the fact that they live with their mother and visit daddy every other weekend.

Once they enter kindergarten or first grade, they realize that their family is different from other families. Perhaps they miss having their dad around more often, and will once again mourn that loss as they re-process what has happened to them. It is at this time that the child will have the ability to grieve more completely. That is, they can actually reach a point of acceptance of their family situation, even though it has not changed in years. You see, a child cannot really mourn the loss until they can understand what it is that they have lost.

This does not mean that your child's grieving is over. As we will see in Chapter Seven, the effects can last a lifetime. The reactions can range from mild to severe whenever this child prepares to enter a new stage of their life. The transition from pre-teen to teenage years can provide a whole new set of insecurities. Teenage to adulthood can require additional support needs; as in the classic question, "Who's going to help me pay for college?".

Then when they begin to think about marriage, or having children, there are a whole new set of questions and adjustments which usually emerge. These adjustments, however, are well beyond the scope of your child's immediate reaction to your divorce. These are considered "long term adjustments" and will be discussed more fully in our next chapter.

School Age Children

For the school aged child there is an increasing awareness of the extent of the loss in their lives. Therefore, there is an increasing ability to reach a point of acceptance. This does not mean that some of the children who witness their parents break-up while in this age range do not have a *delayed reaction*. Some do! However, many are able to reach acceptance within a couple of years, and then honestly handle the "mini-crises" as they occur throughout their lives.

At the lower end of this age range (ages 6–8), children will return to youthful play, fantasy daydreaming, and child-like trust as part of their acceptance. At the upper age range (ages 8–12), particularly the girls, you will see these children begin to take on increased responsibilities, and at times, act very adult-like. It is therefore, important that you keep in mind that they are still children. You may be tempted to treat them like adults; giving them more responsibilities, expecting adult-like decision making, and maybe even confiding in them. Foster their independence, but don't fall into the trap of robbing them of their childhood.

Other signs of acceptance within this age range can include: a restoration of self confidence and personal security, a return to "normal" scholastic achievement, the ability to focus on new and/or renewed friendships, and an acceptance of the new family structure so that few, if any, emotional adjustments occur whenever your former spouse visits or calls. Within all of these changes the key ingredient is the fact that your child is now able to cope with the changes in their life. They are facing their situation with a sense of acceptance and restored hope.

Teenagers

For teenagers it is sometimes very difficult to recognize when they are in acceptance. This is because they are usually going through so many adjustments and transitions that it is hard to figure out when they are being typical teenagers, and when they are experiencing anger or depression over the divorce. Therefore, it is not uncommon for this age group to experience a prolonged grieving period. This can last until the teenager comes to a point of stability in their lives. When you combine the turbulence of puberty with the trauma of divorce, you can see how acceptance can be so elusive.

Some teenagers, however, do make the necessary adjustments. They may continue to struggle, and experience pain, but they are able to cope with their new situation. Some of the evidence that this is taking place can include:

1. Your teenager is able to talk to you or someone else about what they are experiencing. The key element here is that they are able to honestly and accurately describe the circumstances of the divorce and their emotions.

2. For the most part, forgiveness has taken place, so that even though your teen may know that one or both parents were at fault, they no longer blame or resent that person.

3. Even though your teen may not be able to express their love, there is a re-establishment of a loving relationship. One in which there is a rebuilding of trust taking place. (Some parents would swear that this is impossible until they reach adulthood.)

4. Your teen should show signs of risk taking, such as reaching out in new relationships. Risk taking involves facing your fears or insecurities, and moving forward anyway. Therefore, knowledge is gained. Parents

should notice evidence that some personal growth is taking place. (As opposed to regression.)

5. Last but not least, there needs to be some sign of personal responsibility before your teen can truly be considered to be in acceptance. This does not mean that your child is taking any of the responsibility for the divorce itself, but they need to move beyond blaming their parents or others for *most* of their problems. Instead, your teen should show signs of at least beginning to take responsibility for their own actions and reactions. They hopefully gain an accurate sense of control over their recovery process. Since this ability requires higher level reasoning skills, it usually increases as your child develops and matures.

Adults

It may seem surprising, but adults experience the same depth of pain and grieving as do the children, when their parents split up. Many parents have told me that they choose to wait until their children are older and perhaps out of the house before separating. They are surprised to find that their children still go through the same grieving process, even though they were seemingly a lot less dependant on their parents.

Assuming their lives are somewhat stabilized, (that means they are not "21 going on 13") the adult children of divorcing parents tend to recover within the two year time frame and show signs of acceptance more quickly than the younger children or the teenagers. The list of signs of acceptance are similar if not identical to the list found in the "teenage" section. The major difference is the amount of time involved. Since adults are better able to understand adult-like motivations and behaviors, they are more apt to accept and forgive *after* they have worked through their own grieving. One word of caution however. Your adult children are much more likely to figure out what "really happened" even though you may not tell them. They are less likely to see one parent as totally right and the other as wrong. They probably see fault on both sides, even though they might side totally with you when they are in your presence. This is commonly known as "buttering both sides of your bread", or learning political savvy. This is not necessarily negative though, since this is a natural reaction to being caught in the middle.

Helping Your Child Reach Acceptance

I believe that you can't really speed up the recovery time, but you *can* reduce the pain involved by making some wise decisions. I also believe that you can *prolong* the recovery time by making some poor choices, such as using your children to get back at the other parent, prolonging the hostilities, or dating before you or the children are emotionally ready. These, and many other errors of judgement, are actually quite common among parents who are divorcing.

It is important for you to keep in mind that *the greatest predictor of your children reaching a point of acceptance is for you as a parent to reach acceptance first.* You see, children don't typically recover in an atmosphere where a parent continues to get angry or fight over co-parenting issues. They also do not do well in an environment where depression, gloom and hopelessness are pervasive. Therefore, you need to do whatever it takes to make *yourself* healthy, and then concentrate on helping your children. I have heard parents say to me that they couldn't go to a divorce recovery program because they didn't want to spend the time away from their children. Or that they probably need counseling, but would rather spend the money to get counseling for their children, since their kids are their priority.

Although I can admire the intention of these parents, I also know that it doesn't help the child to work on recovery issues and then walk into a home atmosphere where there is an unforgiving spirit. Acceptance needs to be modeled to kids *first* from their parents.

This does not mean that you cannot show weakness or vulnerability with your children. In fact, some signs of healthy grieving can be very helpful to kids. One single mother recently told me about her struggle to not cry in front of her children. She wanted to appear to be strong and healed even though she was working through a lot of sorrow.

I told her that I thought it would be good for her to let her children see her cry. "They need to see the healthy expression of emotion, and to know that it is okay".

"On the other hand", I continued to explain to her, "you don't want to demonstrate hysterical, uncontrollable crying. They can benefit from seeing you struggle a bit, but they also need to know that you are still in control. At least in control enough for them to feel secure in their dependance upon you".

Honesty seems to be a key in the expression of your emotions with your children. Explain to them how you are feeling and where you are in the recovery process. Don't tell them you are in acceptance when you know you are not. You don't want to lie to yourself or to your children about how you are feeling emotionally.

You may, however, want to push yourself a bit for the sake of the kids. By this I mean you may want to give in or give up on some of your own issues (For example, the need to get even.) so that everyone involved can get on with their lives. This is good for you as well as the children.

A good example of this would be the Morgan family. There is no question about the fact that Mrs. Morgan had been "dumped". She had put her husband through medical school, and now that he was becoming a prominent doctor, he left his wife for a younger woman. This is an unfortunate, yet all too common scenario. I can sure empathize with Mrs. Morgan's hostility and desire for vindication. Yet when she and her two children arrived at my office some two years after the break-up, I was struck by how destructive *both* parents had been to their children. They had returned to court several times over custody and financial battles. And now, once again, Mrs. Morgan was thinking of going to court for more support.

After talking extensively with her two children, I recognized that they had both suffered *extreme* heartache because of their being used as pawns in most of the legal battles. Even though their parents desired to leave them out of it, the kids inevitably heard the venom that each side was going to use during the next legal round.

Acknowledging the amount of time that had past (two years) and the devastating effects on the children, I recommended that she examine her motives for going back into court, and to try to avoid the litigation if at all possible. As we discussed the matter further it became obvious to both of us that she needed to let go of her need to "make him pay". In turn, I assured her that both she and her children would be better off.

As you move on with your life, and especially if things begin to go well, you will begin to recognize the value in *forgiving* your ex. Forgiveness is necessary whether or not the other party asks for it. In fact, for the majority there is never a time when the "erring party" comes back with his or her tail between their legs, requesting that you forgive them. No—that only happens in your dreams. The truth is that we need to forgive the other party in spite of their actions toward us because it is what truly sets us free to more on with our lives. And for the sake of our children, we need to move on! (See Appendix re: Divorce Recovery)

The true test of forgiveness comes when you're not doing well, and it seems like your ex is prospering. Then, even the most kind-hearted soul steams inside, fanaticizing about how they might hasten their ex's downfall. I'm reminded of the single parent who told me that she loaded her kids up with sugar and caffeine before sending them over to visit with their dad and his new wife! (I hope I haven't given any of you new ideas.)

Since it is inevitable that these feelings will continue to haunt you, your decision to forgive must be ongoing. In other words, you must continually choose to ignore or let go of those nagging concerns and pitfalls. Your children will see how you choose to handle the minor crises that come up, and will learn appropriate responses to life's little traumas.

CHAPTER SUMMARY

In this chapter we have looked at the final stage of adjustment that children of divorce experience—Acceptance. This last stage can take two years or more to reach. We have defined this stage as the point at which your child is able to deal honestly with their new lifestyle, and begin to move forward in new and more healthy directions. This adjustment is different within various age groups, but is universally marked by the child's ability to be satisfied with their new family. Their defenses are lowered, and they are able to begin taking risks again in significant relationships.

Once your child reaches acceptance this does not mean that they will not slip back into another period of adjustment. In fact, it is typical, particularly for younger children, to go through all of the stages of grieving each time they approach a new developmental stage, or significant transition in their life. This is considered by many to be a "delayed reaction", or to be just part of the long term effects of the divorce. These long term effects will be the subject of our next chapter.

Chapter 7

The Long Term Effects

Cindy was a girl who had problems with relationships. She had broken off four serious relationships in two years. For each of them, the pattern was always the same. Cindy would grow closer and closer, until there came a point where some type of commitment was implied. Then the difficulties would start. The specifics were different each time, but the basic issues were always the same.

Cindy's partners couldn't be trusted. Or at least according to Cindy they couldn't be trusted. You see, she would usually set up some type of trap in which she tested the character of her beau. Sometimes it would be checking and re-checking his whereabouts even though he would tell her where he would be. Other times it was merely whether or not he could account for all of his time when asked, "What did you do today?"

I can remember one specific incident in which Cindy was incensed by her boyfriends "dishonesty". It seems that when she asked him about what he had done that day, he failed to mention that he had called for her earlier in the evening and talked briefly with her roommate. From that point on, Cindy became suspicious that there was something going on between her boyfriend and her roommate. Needless to say the relationship did not last much longer, and her friendship with her roommate remained extremely strained.

Cindy, who is now 25 years old, came into counseling to find out why she seemed to have such poor luck in relationships, particularly with men. As you may have guessed, Cindy came from a divorced home. She first found out about her fathers indiscretions when she was about 10. Her parents did not divorce right away, but rather, Cindy remembers a series of incidents in which her mom and dad had prolonged arguments over suspected affairs. Finally, when she was 17, Cindy's parents got a divorce. Her mom continually reminded Cindy about how devious her father had been, even though Cindy still saw him a couple of times a month.

This is a typical example of a divorce which has long term implications. Today we are seeing more and more published about the long term effects of divorce on individuals. In one of the more popular works on this topic, Judith Wallerstein followed children of divorce for over fifteen years. (*See Appendix*). This book, along with many follow-up articles and books, seem to have given adult children of divorce the courage to come forward in order to tell their stories. The comments I hear repeatedly proclaim, "I'm glad someone is finally recognizing and documenting the long term effects of divorce. It has had a significant impact on our lives and relationships". In fact, one of the greatest proofs that I have found for the impact of divorce on children, is in talking to the adult children of divorce. Every one of them, and I've talked to hundreds, have said, "I'll do everything I can to be sure I don't do this to my children." The sad truth is that children of divorce actually have a slightly higher divorce rate than the rest of the population.

Many of you are probably aware of the huge interest there is today for support groups for those who have come from dysfunctional families. These groups most frequently include adult children of alcoholics, adult children of incest and abuse; and now, more and more we are seeing adult children of divorce as one of the recovery groups offered. (See Appendix re: Adult Children). At our own counseling center, just the mention of such a support group will usually initiate many calls of interest from potential participants. As one caller recently stated, "I know my parents divorce, and following years of conflict, have effected me. I'm not quite sure of all of the

ways I have been effected, but I'd love to talk
to others who have been through the same
type of experience. Just to know that I'm not
alone in my feelings, and to gain insights into
some of my behaviors would be well worth
it".

Long Term vs. Short Term

Many would ask, "What's the difference between long term and short term effects of
divorce?". As discussed in previous chapters,
the short term effects of divorce are those
reactions which begin immediately and can
last for a number of years. The short term
reactions don't truly end, however, until the
child reaches a point of acceptance. Beyond
that, even though the child has worked
through the grieving of their family break up,
they still have to work through the implications of growing up in a divorced home. These
effects, which are what I consider to be the
long term effects, have been documented to
last up to fifteen years for some adult children
of divorce, and may very well be permanent.

If you remember from Chapter Three when
I discussed the three main categories of reaction for children, I mentioned that approximately one third of the children of divorce
never seem to recover from the trauma of
their parents divorce. (The actual figures are
37–41% depending on the research you read.)
These are the most seriously effected of the

children of divorce, both from a long term and short term perspective. For these children, the reactions included in chapters four through six are what they tend to live with for the rest of their lives. They don't learn healthy coping skills, and therefore, lead a lifestyle of continuing struggle, depression, anxiety, difficulty in personal relationships, and other problem behaviors.

The children who, after a period of adjustment, are able to cope and move on with their lives (approximately 63%) are the ones who seem quite normal to those around them, and outwardly lead healthy, productive lives. Yet as is true for all of us, what they grew up with has a large effect on how they live today. Divorce shapes our personalities and character; our interests and ambitions. These are the subtle changes that will be covered as part of the long term effects of divorce on children. As might be expected, this will only be a general review of the research, and a personal review of my experiences. Time and practicality do not permit us to discuss all of the subtle changes that take place with your children. That would require volumes. You can merely observe your own children to see how they are changed over time.

Factors To Be Considered

There are a number of factors to be considered when discussing how your children will be effected over the long term. Let me list a few of the more prevalent factors.

1. *The age of the child at the time of the divorce.* Researchers estimate that most of your child's personality is developed by the age of six. This does not mean that there are not changes in their personalities beyond that time, but for those children who witness their parents break up at a young age, there is a greater chance that it will have an effect on their personalities. It stands to reason that the longer your child lives in a single parent or blended family, the more likely it will effect their personalities. This does not have to be a frightening statistic for those of you who have young children. It merely indicates that you will need to be even more aware of how your child might be effected, and how you might compensate for specific losses. (Note: Most of the long term studies have started with young children, and therefore, may be overly pessimistic, since these children spent a greater percentage of their lives in a divorced home.)

2. *The number of changes which result from the divorce.* The impact of divorce upon children is greater when you add on other life stresses, such as moving to a new home, new church, new school district, add a new spouse to the picture, or try to blend a family. All of these changes are difficult for children if they are experienced by themselves, but when they are heaped together, as is the case in many

divorcing situations, the effects can be life-
long. Wherever possible, parents need to control the number of changes, and perhaps even
make sacrifices in order to limit the upheaval.

3. *The adjustment of the custodial parent
in the divorce.* While both parents are of key
importance in the eventual well being of the
children, research indicates that the emotional health of the custodial parent (usually
mom) is the greatest predictor of the children's adjustment. Therefore, it is important
for both parents to get the help that they need
to resolve the anger, resentment, depression,
or anxiety produced by the divorce, and to
conclude any ongoing squabbles as quickly as
possible. Almost all couples have conflicts
during the early stages of the divorce. But if
these continue beyond the actual divorce settlement, they can suck all participants back
into the blackhole of divorce for more years
than is necessary.

Since the children spend the majority of
their time with the custodial parent, it stands
to reason that their attitudes will influence
the children. No matter what the circumstances, the custodial parent must choose an
attitude of reconciliation and one that desires
whatever is best for the children, particularly
when it comes to the relationship with the
other parent.

4. *The relationship with the non-custodial
parent.* For years we have tended to ignore the

importance of the relationship with the non-custodial parent (usually dad). Within the past five years or so, we have seen more and more research which points to the fact that the non-custodial parent is also a key player. (Any of you dads out there who might be thinking about giving up on seeing your kids, please read this very carefully.) Many researchers have found that a primary reason for negative effects of divorce on children was the loss of contact with one of the parents (usually dad). And in fact, the traditional visiting pattern of every other weekend, has created feelings of intense dissatisfaction, and at times reactive depression among children, particularly the boys.

Consistent and frequent contact with the noncustodial parent has repeatedly been shown to correlate with well adjusted children, unless the father is abusive or otherwise unfit. The relationship with father has been linked to identity with the opposite sex for girls, ambition and motivation for boys, and overall adjustment and relating abilities for both sexes. The well being of the child has proven to be particularly strong when the custodial mother encouraged the continued contact with father.

If the relationship with the non-custodial parent is so important, then why is it that two years after the divorce, only 40% of the dad's have regular visits with their children? This is an alarming and discouraging statistic. Having talked with many fathers who have actually "given up", I have found that many become discouraged by their lack of input into the child's upbringing. To put it in their words, "Why should I continue paying, when I have little or no say in how the kids are raised." This is perhaps the reason joint custody arrangements have a much higher rate of involvement by the father. When they have more input, they are more likely to stay involved, and therefore, more likely to have well adjusted children.

5. *Other specific traumas which accompany the divorce.* The research for this is incomplete, but it is my opinion that most of the children of divorce who fall into the one third of the children who never seem to recover from their parents' divorce are also the ones who have to contend with other specific traumas. These traumas include but are not limited to physical abuse, sexual abuse, severe emotional or verbal abuse, extended neglect, drug or alcohol addiction of one or both parents, and mental illness in the family. For children exposed to these factors, the long term implications of divorce are greatly complicated by pre-existing conditions and compounding problems. Once again, this is a general statement, and therefore, does not imply that if your child was exposed to one or more of these traumas, that they will end up a

basket case. This factor merely indicates a greater propensity for long term problems, and therefore, you need to be particularly sensitive to your child's needs and emotional condition.

The Long Term Effects

Jason, who is now 24, first came to see me when he was 15. At that time he had long hair (which was a little more in style then), torn jeans, a punk rock T-shirt, and a sour look on his face. Jason was actually referred to me by his mom because he had decided to drop out of school. Mom said she would permit it (she had actually lost her ability to control him anymore) if he would go to three counseling sessions.

Imagine yourself in my position. Here's this big, 15 year old punk rocker, sitting in your office, glaring at you, as if to say "I dare you to get through to me". He didn't want to be there, and to be honest, I didn't either.

Every topic I brought up was met with silence, or an occasional "yep" or "nope" (mostly "nope's"). Finally, I decided that my only option, and one that I found would work as a last resort, was to talk to him about something *he* was interested in—music. Not just any music, but punk rock and heavy metal music. Now you have to understand that I hate, and never listen to punk rock or heavy metal music. In fact, I encourage parents to keep it away from their kids. But in this case, I felt it was my only way to connect.

Suddenly Jason became very animated and talkative. He was surprised that I had shown any interest. (Believe me, it was tough.) He later stated that no other adult had ever taken interest in this topic, which he valued so highly. Adults usually walked away or told him to turn it off. Jason went on to tell me about all the groups, the most popular songs, and the meaning behind the lyrics. (As if anyone could actually hear the words.) He then offered to bring his tape player next week, along with a couple of his favorite tapes.

Well I survived his tapes, and to make a long story short, Jason continued coming, by choice, for the next six months. During that time, he began to tell me about his family, his life, and his feelings. Jason was a very angry young man. His father had left the home when he was about nine years old, and moved in with another woman. The new woman had children of her own and was soon pregnant with Jason's soon to be step-brother. As dad gradually broke off contact (and financial support) with his former family, Jason felt more rejection, resentment, and then anger with each week. He eventually withdrew emotionally, and instead, isolated himself in his room with his music and an occasional marijuana cigarette.

Jason's main problem was his attitude and motivation. He had given up on life by the time he was 14. After all, life wasn't fair, and he couldn't even sustain his fathers love. This inability to have a sense of control over his own life is what researchers have identified in approximately 45% of the male children of divorce. As in the case of Jason, even though the child might be intelligent and talented, there is a higher tendency for them to show little direction or purpose in their lives. Dropping out of school, not attending college, bumbling their way through college, and being under employed after school, are all typical signs of the phenomenon in the male, and a few female, children of divorce.

Today, Jason works in a factory. He finished high school, but went no further even though he has above average intelligence. He is socially active, and appears to be much happier today. His hair is still long, but fortunately his taste in music has moderated. To his friends, he's an average 24 year old, and a nice guy. But to me, he is a victim; a victim of divorce.

Alice is a 26 year old adult child of divorce. Her parents split up when she was seven, and she gradually lost contact with her father over a period of two years. Her mother remarried within that two year time period, but was divorced again when Alice was eleven. Since the second divorce, Alice's mom has had a series of boyfriends, but has not remarried again. At the time of both divorces, after a period of adjustment, Alice seemed to come through them fairly well. It was in adolescence, as is often the case, that Alice began to have difficulties. She found her first "true love" when she was fifteen, and was convinced that they would eventually marry. When that relationship broke off, Alice, in disgust, found that she could get boys to do what *she* wanted them to do, through sex. Throughout high school and college, Alice was sexually active, but soon after graduation had a "born again" experience which led her into a new lifestyle. She became active in a church single's group, and now believes in a heavenly Father who loves her unconditionally, and for whom she does not have to perform. The new difficulty is in finding that same kind of loving relationship with a viable man.

Whether it is the reaction found in Alice, or the lack of trust found in the example of Cindy (from the first paragraph of this chapter), researchers have documented this "sleeper effect" in approximately 66% of the female children of divorce. This has been called the sleeper effect because surprisingly, it has been found quite often in the women who previously seemed to be doing the best. It occurs most frequently at a time when women are making important decisions about their lives. In this way, it is similar to the reaction in young men.

The common element in the sleeper effect, as seen in the two women presented, is fear. Fear of commitment and fear of betrayal. For some, the fear may lead to the coping strategy of control. In other words, "If I can learn how to control men or the situation, then I won't be hurt again." I have seen this numerous times in the lives of adult children. While I can empathize with the feeling, I'm afraid the coping strategy can become quite unhealthy.

Another coping strategy which is used by both men and women who are experiencing the sleeper effect, is avoidance. This can include avoidance of significant relating, or avoidance of any kind of commitment. Usually, patterns of relating are developed, and unconsciously repeated, in which relationships only reach a certain level, and then "self destruct" before they can go any further. This can include an inability to communicate deeper than a superficial level, an inability to make a commitment, or an inability to allow the relationship to grow beyond a friendship or a purely sexual basis.

The combination of control and avoidance can reach extreme levels among some adult children of divorce. This is evidenced by a disproportionately high number of both men and women who are sexually acting out, homosexual, in treatment facilities for personality disorders, and who experience divorce in their own marriages in spite of vows that it will never happen to them. Without insights into their pattern of relating, and help in overcoming these patterns, these difficulties may well follow them the rest of their lives.

Another documented long term effect of divorce is commonly referred to as the "overburdened child". When marriage breaks down it is common for both the mother and the father to do less parenting. The mother, or custodial parent, is often worn down by the changes in her life, including moves, job changes, new financial responsibilities, and parenting alone. The father, who feels guilt because he is not there for the kids as often as he'd like to be, just wants their times together to be enjoyable. Therefore, both parents tend to discipline less, spent less time with their children, and may be less sensitive to their needs. They themselves may be struggling with their own reactions and recovery.

Unable to meet the challenges of parenting as a single, many parents begin to lean on their children to pick up the slack. We have all heard of the "latch key" kid, who must take major responsibilities in the home well before they might otherwise have to. The child's role may include, housekeeping, babysitting younger siblings, being the "man

of the house", becoming the mediator in arguments, being the parents' confidant, and emotionally supporting the parent. While most of
this is not intentional, it is a fact of life in
many single parent families.

The first time I met Sarah, I was amazed at
what a responsible, mature child she was for
being only fourteen. Her mother was quite
proud of the fact that teachers and friends all
commented on what a good job she had done
in raising her daughter all alone. The presenting problem was that they were having difficulty in choosing a college. (Most kids are not
even thinking about college at age fourteen.)
Even though it was early, Sarah was anticipat-
ing a problem when it came time for her to go
away to school. You see, she wanted to go
away for school. Her mother on the other
hand felt that she should stay home so that
she could continue to provide the proper guidance to her daughter.

Since college was still three years away, and
Sarah was so responsible, I was confused as to
why this was such a burning issue. As we
explored it further, it became evident that the
reason mom needed Sarah to stay home was
to help mother "keep it together". Sarah was
the one who kept the house in order. She
prepared the evening meal, and then would
ask mom all about her day when she got
home from work. Sarah did not go out socially
during the week or on weekends because she

didn't want her mother to be all alone at home. If mom did happen to go out on a date, which was rare, she always solicited Sarah's approval on her choices because, she stated, "Sarah's a better judge of character than I am."

Whenever she returned from her dates, she would confide in Sarah everything that she liked and didn't like about the person so that together they could come to some conclusion about any future relationship. The truth of the matter was that if Sarah went away to college, neither one of them were sure if mom could make it on her own. Talk about role reversals!

Sarah is a good example of the overburdened child. The child's role becomes instrumental to the well being of the parent. The divorce itself may not be to blame, but serves as a catalyst for bringing to the surface specific emotional difficulties. As with any type of dysfunctional family, the results of the child taking on so much responsibility, so early in life, is generally twofold. Either they react by going the opposite way and become overly irresponsible, or they continue in their overburdened lifestyle, and therefore, are at risk for perfectionism, nervous breakdowns, overly nurturing relationships, over-parenting, and losing their own identity for a cause or another person. (See Appendix re: Codependency)

Preliminary studies have indicated that approximately 15% of the children of divorce are overburdened. Some have indicated, however, that this estimate is low, since there are increased responsibilities for nearly all of the children of divorce. As we shall see in the next section, a balance of responsibility may be the key, since increased responsibility can actually have a positive impact on some of the children of divorce.

Whether it is the "diminished motivation", the "sleeper effect", or the "overburdened child" syndrome, it is hard to point the only finger of blame at the divorce. Divorce never stands alone as a one time traumatic event, but is experienced in a continuum which begins with an unhappy marriage, goes through custody battles and court hearings, and begin ripple effects that continue for generations: The biblical phrase from Exodus chapter 20, comes to mind; "The sins of the father are passed on through many generations."

Do these predictions of gloom mean that parents should stay together for the sake of the children? Even though the research is troubling and needs to be taken seriously, there are situations in which continuing the marriage would be intolerable. And to stay in a bad situation for the sake of the children would probably only lead to more resentment and possible violence. Even though there are very few comparisons of children from divorced homes with children from unhappy homes, all known evidence points to the fact that children exposed to parental fighting and the pressure of relentless conflict, turn out to be less well adjusted than many of the children of divorce.

If divorce is undertaken with thoughts of the children's well being, and if both parents work together for the sake of the kids, then there are many things which can be done to lessen the negative effects of the divorce on your children. These practical guidelines will be the focus of the next section of the book, but first let's turn our attention to a much more positive topic.

Positive Effects

It is hard to believe that anyone could write anything positive about divorce. In fact, in reviewing the literature, it is hard to find anything of a positive nature. But if divorce is viewed as a handicap to children, then we must look at the fact that many have taken the worst kinds of handicaps and used them to build character and personality which becomes the envy of others. So it is with the long term effects of divorce. I have met with many teenagers and adults who have shared how their parents divorce has been used to build strength of character and moral resolve into their personalities.

As Janet, a sixteen year old child of divorce, explained it to me:

> It is hard to find anything positive that can come out of the divorce when it first happens. My dad left when I was only six, and I know that it has been difficult on me and my mom. But I wouldn't trade anything for the things that I have learned from growing up in a single parent household. I have been forced to face the realities of life at an early age. Realities like . . . life isn't always easy, and that there are no guarantees in life. These things have forced me to be more practical and down to earth. I know that I'm a more responsible and resourceful person today because of the divorce.

Crystal, a seventeen year old, echoed similar comments;

> "Yeah, it definitely takes time, but you do work through it, and when you do, you find that you are much more understanding than other kids your age. You have to be! After all, you've seen your parents fail. Everything they taught you has fallen apart. So now you have to decide how you're going to live your life. What are you going to believe in. For me, it has strengthened my faith in God. He is real in my life, not because my parents told me so, but because I needed a source of strength which was greater than me, and greater than my parents. I've found that now,

so I consider myself luckier than other kids my age."

David, a seventeen year old survivor of two divorces, put it this way:

Something about the divorce forces you to view life differently. It somehow puts every other life event in perspective. When your mom or dad leave you at age five, and your whole world seems to fall apart, then you are better able to deal with other crises as they occur. You're perhaps wiser and more mature. For example, I see some of my classmates who fall apart over bad grades or College Boards or something. You even read about kids who kill themselves because they didn't get accepted to the college of their choice. Things like that upset me, but I know it's not the end of the world. I always figure to myself, you've survived your parents divorce, you can certainly get through this one.

Here are some of the common themes that I have heard when interviewing children of divorce about the positive aspects of divorce. First and foremost, they all indicate that there is *nothing* good about it in the beginning. But over a long period of time, some of the following characteristics may emerge:

1. *Children of divorce are more sensitive to other kids and their problems.* It stands to reason that when you've been through a sig-

nificant life trauma and have felt like no one else understands your pain, once you work through that, you are bound to be more compassionate to other people and the difficulties they might face. I have seen this first hand whenever our counseling center sponsors a program to help others who are struggling with some life crisis. Adult and teenage children of divorce are among the first to volunteer to help.

Julie, a sixteen year old girl expressed it like this, "Having cried myself to sleep many times, I realize the depth of pain a little girl can feel. Now, when I have the opportunity to share my healing with someone else who is struggling, I feel like it was almost worth it. A lot of my friends come to me with their problems, because they say I understand them and can really relate. You know, I think they're right. But it's taken a long time for me to get to the point where I can help anyone."

2. *Children of divorce tend to be more mature and responsible then their peers.* Even though this maturity comes from the "school of hard knocks", many of the children of divorce that I have spoken with, seem to have a wisdom beyond their years. This comes from having to grapple with issues that other kids don't have to face until they are much older. Issues like loyalty, betrayal, adultery, child support, court hearings, rejection, etc. Although you would probably prefer to have

your children avoid these issues, they do help the child move from concrete to abstract reasoning.

One teenage boy put it this way, "I used to just think about me and my needs. Now I'm more concerned for my little brother. I've tried to come along side of him and support him through this mess because I know how much I hurt when I was his age. I sometimes just take him fishing or something so we can get away and talk. We cry together, laugh together. . . . we're closer now than ever."

Additionally, since your child inevitably takes on more responsibilities, they either fight the changes, or eventually become more responsible people. They stop blaming, or looking to others for the solution to their problems, and realize that they've got to take responsibility for their own futures. Many people don't learn this until they are adults, but the "pressure cooker" of divorce has a way of maturing a child quicker than might otherwise be expected.

Margie, a seventeen year old, said, "Before the divorce, my life was fairly secure. Everything was taken care of as far as my schooling, my welfare, and even my future. Then, when everything fell apart, I learned that the world wasn't secure at all. (While in high school) I had to work, take care of my brothers and sisters, cook, and clean. I feel like I got a taste of motherhood.

I'm leaving for college soon, and I know that I'm going to have to work my way through, but I know I'll value my education more, and not take things for granted as much. After all, it's my education and my future."

This increased level of responsibility may include the child's moral development. Children of divorce are faced with their parents moral failures; lies, manipulations, maybe even cheating and stealing. Obviously, this forces the child to think more about what they believe and how they are going to live their lives. It is no longer enough to believe something because "my mother told me so".

After a sometimes rebellious transition, children of divorce settle down to a belief system which is based on what they have concluded about life, rather than what their parents have taught them. Even though this may be a scary thought to parents, it is actually a more mature and enduring belief system than one based on the beliefs of the parents. Nancy explained it this way, "All my life my parents taught me right and wrong. Then I saw my mom and dad break just about every one of their own rules. It forced me to really examine what was truth. Today, I have a strong faith in God which helps me in every area of my life".

3. *Children of divorce are better able to put life experiences into a proper perspective.*

John said it this way, "When you've been through some of the worst things that can happen in life at age eight, everything else that comes your way seems so much easier. You've survived divorce and so now you're determined that nothing else is going to get you down again. I still have difficult times, but I always go back to my parents divorce and compare it to that. Then I know I'm going to be just fine."

Growing up in a storybook life many times leaves us with the expectation that we are going to "live happily ever after". It can be a real shocker when we discover that the fairy tale is not true. I have seen adults come apart because they were not prepared for the realities of life; realities that children of divorce learn much earlier. Even though we would rather shield our kids from such difficulties, they have a way of teaching lessons that last a lifetime.

4. *Children of divorce are very motivated to succeed in marriage.* Having experienced first hand the effects of divorce, the children usually become determined that it won't happen to them. Even deeper than this determination is the realization that you can't take certain things for granted, such as someone's love.

Having grown up in a happy, secure home environment, it wasn't until after college that I learned that the world isn't always a fair place and that bad things *do* happen to good

people. This was a difficult lesson which
many of us learned after stumbling into relationships with people who we thought were
trustworthy and good. Children of divorce
learn at a very young age that good people
(their parents) still hurt them and perhaps
can't be trusted. When looking for a mate,
they tend to be much more cautious.

This is the positive side of the finding that
children of divorce (especially women) tend to
delay marriage because of their fear of betrayal. This may be healthy if we consider
that they may avoid a future divorce by not
marrying the first man they fall in love with.
In fact, there is some preliminary evidence in
Judith Wallerstein's longitudinal study which
suggests that even though children of divorce
are afraid of commitment, they eventually
settle into relationships that last. She says,
"I'm predicting that after a lot of trial and
error, after a lot of getting hurt, a significant
number of children of divorce will find a relationship that will stick".

When I interviewed teenagers of divorce for
this book, I asked the question, "How do you
think your future will be effected, particularly your getting married?" Everyone of
them responded that they would be more cautious about who they chose to marry. This
usually included a list of qualities that they
would need to see. One teen put it this way, "I
don't mean to be picky, but I know that I want

to know someone for a long time before I marry them. I want to be sure they're not going to change later on. I want a guy who is kind and compassionate, but most important, someone who has a strong faith in God and knows the meaning of commitment."

One parent summed this point up best; "If my divorce helps to keep my daughter from having to go through the same thing someday, then it was worth it!"

CHAPTER SUMMARY

In this chapter we have taken a look at some of the long term effects of divorce on children; both positive and negative. We have seen some of the important factors which determine your child's adjustment over the long term, and made some suggestions to both moms and dads on how they can effect their own child's healthy recovery. Even though there are probably hundreds of ways in which the child's personality is effected by divorce, we took a specific look at three of the most commonly cited effects. These included a lack of motivation and direction in the lives of approximately 40% of the young men whose parents divorced; difficulty in relationships among approximately 66% of the young women in the study; and an "overburdened child" syndrome found in about 15% of the adult children of divorce.

While these effects are troubling to read about, we also examined some of the positive outcomes which can result from a divorce. The strength of character and resiliency which has been demonstrated by many children of divorce is an encouragement and challenge to us all.

As we move into the next section which deals with helping your child recover in the most healthy way, we all need to remember the part of the Serenity Prayer which states, "God, grant me . . . the courage to change the things I need to change. . .".

SECTION THREE

HELPING YOUR CHILD

Chapter 8

Breaking the News

"I was five or six when I first remember my parents fighting a lot. I remember that dad was working more and more, and that I missed him. There were times when dad was gone for weeks at a time. When we asked my mom where dad was, she would always say, 'Away on a business trip'. I now know that my dad and mom were separated. Whenever they tried to reconcile, my mom would say that dad was home for a vacation. This went on for about two years. It didn't matter what my mom said anymore. My brother and I knew there was something wrong and we knew that we didn't like it. When mom finally told us the truth, that she and dad were getting a divorce, it was only because he was getting married to someone else, and wanted my brother and I to be in the wedding.

I wish my mom had told us the truth two years earlier. Then we could have started the

grieving process, and maybe been more accepting of our new stepmother and step-sister. That was really tough for us to swallow."
—a fourteen year old boy.

The first place you want to begin to intervene with your children, is as soon as the possibility of divorce is apparent. For most of you it is already too late to undo the way the news was broken to your children, but if possible, this is where you and your spouse will want to start. Kids usually know that there is something going on long before you give them credit for knowing. It is also my experience that they know and understand more than you think.

The example at the beginning of this chapter is obviously not the way to break the news to your children, but it is hard to tell each one of you how to handle your particular situation. This whole section on "helping your child" will tend to sound like a cookbook of do's and don'ts. Keep in mind that I am presenting a list of guidelines, some of which you can implement, and some of which you can't.

Remember our prayer: "God, grant me the serenity to accept the things that I cannot change, the courage to change the things that I can, and the wisdom to know the difference". Also keep in mind that there are no secret formulas, or even standard methods of operation. Your child is an individual, and therefore, you will need to tailor this information to best fit your situation, and your child.

Speak the Truth in Love

In the book of Ephesians, the Apostle Paul writes that we are to "speak the truth in love". This is the best way that I can describe the communication that should take place between all parties involved in a separation or divorce. This may be near impossible at times, but I believe that it needs to be our goal. Let's explore how this guideline plays itself out by answering some of the most commonly asked questions I hear from divorcing parents.

When should we tell the kids?

I think it is important to tell the kids what is going on as soon as both of you know. If you're just having marital problems, then it is important that you get help, but don't feel compelled to tell the children anything that is of a personal nature between you and your spouse. If the children are older, then they will know that something is not right, and may even know that you are seeing a counselor. If they ask, use this as an opportunity to demonstrate the proper way to handle problems. "Your mother and I are having some personal problems that we need to work out.

Because we are committed to each other and to the family, we want to get help in resolving these problems as quickly as we can." If your children are too young to understand the problem, or if they don't ask, then there is no need to share your personal lives with your kids.

Once the problem reaches a point where divorce or separation is apparent, then it affects the whole family. The children need to be told as soon as it can be arranged. This should only be delayed if you need to work out some of the details or if it happens to fall on an important day such as Christmas or one of the children's birthdays. It is reasonable to wait until some of the details are worked out, such as: Where will mom live? Where will dad live? Where will the kids stay? And how often will we see each parent? You need to present a scenario that is well thought through and which is reassuring to the children if at all possible. If these matters cannot be settled, and it looks like the children are going to find out, you may need to sit them down and tell them as much as you know.

Many parents tend to "protect" their children from the truth as long as possible. One study found that 80% of the preschoolers questioned had received no information about their parents separation. Parents do a disservice to the child by withholding such information. Withholding merely creates anxiety about the future and distrust toward the parent.

How should we tell the kids, and how much should we tell them?

If possible, both parents should sit down with the kids, and together, tell them about the separation or divorce, before one of the parents leaves. If the separation happens abruptly, the parent with the children will need to give them some preliminary information right away, but as soon as it can be arranged, both parents need to come together to tell the children what will happen to the family. This method is important for several reasons. First, with both parents present, there is the greatest possibility of a balanced and honest presentation. Secondly, if the children have any questions, they need to address them to the parent who is best able to answer. And thirdly, the "united front" makes it clear that both parents are in agreement on the decision. This helps to reduce the splitting of loyalties, the playing of one parent against the other, and the fantasy that "my parents will work this out". If one parent is missing, the children are likely to think, "Yeah, that's what mom says, but I know that's not what dad told me".

If one parent is not present, and this is usually the case, then it is important that the parent remember to speak the truth as lovingly as possible. Representing both sides of the issue is very difficult when you are so emotionally involved. Even though you are irate with the other parent, you want to let the children know that it is an issue between the parents, and that you both still love them.

If your child has questions about the other parent, or their reasons for leaving, try to answer his questions as honestly as possible. Don't attribute motives, or make judgements about the other parent. Just state what you know to be true, as nicely as you can. For example:

Don't say- "Your father left because he's irresponsible. He's probably going to be moving in with his girlfriend, and forget all about us".

Try this instead- "Your father loves you very much, but doesn't seem to love me. Even though he does not want to live with me anymore, he wants to visit with you whenever he can".

By taking the "high road", you will end up better off, even if you have good reason to drag your spouse's reputation through the mud. Remember, your children will know the truth sooner or later, and it would be better for you if they remember you as the one who chose the most loving course.

When deciding how much you should tell the kids, you must take into consideration the developmental level of your child. As Carrie put it, "Get the key points across, and then allow for open discussion. If the child knows enough to ask the question, then they're old enough to get an honest answer".

The key points to cover include:

1. How did this happen? What are the reasons?

2. Do you still love me? Does my mother/father still love me? Am I wanted?

3. How will my life be changed? Where will I live, go to school, church, etc.?

4. Am I part of the reason for the break up? Could I have done something to avoid this separation/divorce?

It is most important to cover what will happen to the children. Reassure them of your love for them, and be prepared to back it up with actions. Give the child permission to love *both* parents. For preschoolers it is important that you reassure them that they will be cared for, and then explain the divorce in terms they can understand. For example:

"Mommy loves you very much, and Daddy loves you very much. You are going to live with me, and we will stay in this house where you will eat, sleep and play, just like you do now. Daddy is going to live in an apartment nearby so that he can come and visit you every week. In fact, he will pick you up this Saturday and show you where he lives. You will eat lunch there, and then he will bring you back home where I will be waiting to hear all about your day. We are separating because we don't want to fight anymore. We will all be sad about Daddy leaving, but Mommy and Daddy would be even sadder if Daddy stayed here and we fought a lot".

Children who are elementary age or older need more specific information, particularly about where they will live and the visitation arrangements. They will also require more specifics about what went wrong. You need to be as honest as you can, without discussing anything about sexual problems. If possible, avoid placing blame, since it is true that divorce is rarely all one person's fault.

Don't expect your children to understand your explanations or to ask all of their questions the first time you talk about it. Be prepared to explain the situation and answer questions over and over again. Stress that separation and/or divorce is an adult decision. It was not their fault, nor can they do anything to get the parents get back together. (See Appendix re: Children's Books)

What if the truth is particularly "ugly" or hard to talk about?

I believe it is easier to deal with what we know far better than what we imagine. You need to tell them the truth in as loving a way as you can. The earlier they hear the truth, the sooner they can start to deal with the problem and begin the healing process. You need to use discretion as to the age of the child, and how much they really can understand, but once again, if they are old enough to ask the question, they are old enough to hear an honest answer. For example, if dad is leaving because he has a girlfriend, or he is a homosexual, you may not want to give them all of this information in the first meeting. Soon thereafter, however, you need to tell them what is really going on. Sooner or later, the kids hear the whispers and innuendos, so it is best that they hear it in a straight forward manner from their parents. If possible, the information should come from *dad*, assuming dad is the one with "the problem". In that way they would know that they were hearing first hand information, which is usually more reliable. They would then have opportunity to openly discuss their questions and concerns.

If dad is not available, or not willing to talk with the children, then it obviously falls on the other parent to present as balanced an explanation as possible. Then, if they have questions, you may want to offer to let them discuss the issue with someone a little more neutral. This might be an aunt or uncle they trust, a counselor at the school or the church, or a relative on their father's side, who they might view as being more objective. Your children may not want to do this, but it is important that you at least offer. This allows them the opportunity to seek a "second opinion" without feeling like they are betraying you.

This open communication is one of the key elements in a healthy family. Dysfunctional families are marked by too much interaction, known as enmeshment, too little communication or emotional distancing, and distorted messages, as found in controlling and manipulative families. Healthy interactions allow for open discussion, honest questioning, and invites verification, as when the parent questions their own motives, or encourages the children to get the other parent's point of view.

What about cases where the child is actually abandoned by one of their parents?

When someone apparently abandons their children, it is difficult to speak the truth in a loving way. This is not only because it is hard to be loving in these situations, but because you rarely know what the truth is. I don't believe that you can tell the child that "Daddy doesn't love you", or that "Daddy's not coming back", because there is much evidence to indicate otherwise. Many parents, both mothers and fathers, who apparently abandon their children will later try to contact them and re-establish a relationship. In addition, the fact that they left does not prove their lack of love. Studies have shown that many times the leaving parent feels so bad about themselves that they believe the most loving thing to do is to get out of their families' lives. Their thinking can be so distorted that they feel like the best thing for everyone is that they "disappear".

Therefore, in cases of abandonment, the remaining parent needs to balance their comments so that the children do not have undo hope *or* despair. "I don't know if your father is coming back or not. We need to go on with our lives as if he will never be back, but you never know; he might realize what he is missing someday, and decide to come back to see you."

Another critical reassurance is the child's lovability. "I don't know if your father loves you or not, but I do know that you are a very lovable child. He is not thinking properly right now and has to work through some problems, but I know that if he ever works through those problems he will realize what a wonderful child you are". Or, "I know your father loves you. He just is not able to express it or show it right now because he is trying to figure out his own life. That does not change the fact that you are a wonderful and lovable child. Your father's problems have nothing to do with you."

Aren't children really tougher than we think? In other words, they can eventually recover, no matter how difficult the truth is to hear.

Most children are more resilient than we think. But that does not advocate our "telling all" to the kids. Unfortunately, this idea has often been misinterpreted as meaning "children are more mature than you think." As a result, children are often expected to handle the impact of divorce or other devastating news, with passive serenity. Kids really are tougher than we think in their ability to handle reality when their parents take the time to communicate honestly with them. *Details are seldom necessary, but honesty is critical.*

It is important to remember that one of the casualties of divorce is trust. Trust is destroyed when parents who once said, "We'll always be here for you", are now telling you where daddy will be living. The only way to rebuild your child's trust is through honesty and open communication.

If the truth is too much for your child to handle, they may withdraw or react hysterically. It is natural for parents to back off a bit at that time, and this is probably best. But don't back away from the truth, or indicate that "we might get back together" just to relieve the tension. Eventually, you need to pursue your child in order to encourage them to express their feelings, to "let it all out". To understand the child's feeling and to allow them to express their pain takes great courage on the part of the parent. However, to do so will accelerate acceptance and growth on the part of the child. Further, parents who make the effort to understand and comfort their children usually find that they themselves are comforted.

How can I expect my children to react when we give them the news?

Your child's reaction will vary according to their developmental level and their personality, but generally you can expect some of the following reactions.

1. An under-reaction. This may be a form of denial and the beginning of the grieving process as outlined in Chapter Four. Don't be surprised when your child reacts with, "Can I go out and play now?".

2. A preoccupation with egocentric thoughts. For all the reasons outlined in Chapter Two, your child may react with, "What about my birthday?"; or, "Who's going to take me to Disneyworld?". These are merely concrete expressions of their fear for the future.

3. A lack of interest in the details of the divorce. This reaction may be a reflection of the child's inability to comprehend the news,

and their fear of talking about it. When you ask them if they have questions, it is not unusual for them to express none at the time. Therefore, it is important that you follow-up your initial discussion with other opportunities for the children to express their concerns.

Whatever your child's reaction, it is critical that you continually reassure them, through every stage of their development, that they are loved by both parents, and that the divorce was not their fault. Explaining the separation or divorce to your child cannot really be done in one session. It will require new explanations and reassurances as the child grows and matures. Even as an adult, your child will still have lingering questions that they will need to express. Hopefully, you will create an atmosphere for them which encourages their inquiries.

What if we've already told the children, but we did it all wrong?

I don't believe it's ever too late to go back and do it right. Granted, some of the questions have already been answered, or figured out by the kids, but that doesn't mean that it wouldn't help to have an open discussion about how they feel about all of the changes. You may think that none of these things are an issue for your kids, because they've never mentioned it. That might be because you've never given them permission to talk about it by opening the conversation.

If you've "done it all wrong" by giving the children distorted, bias, or unloving information about the other parent, then I believe it is best to admit your wrongs to the children, ask for their forgiveness, correct the wrongs, and then vow to be more objective and positive in the future.

If possible, and this might really be asking a lot, contact your former spouse to see if he/she might be up for a joint meeting with the children. This could go a long way toward establishing a respectful, cooperative effort in co-parenting the children, which benefits everyone.

CHAPTER SUMMARY

In this chapter, we have examined how to break the news of separation or divorce to your children. We have answered questions regarding when and what to tell the the children. Some of the issues which have been stressed regarding the parents' communication with their children are:

1. To be honest and open in the way you present the information. Give explanations, not defenses or opinions.

2. Focus on what will happen to each child.

Assure them of their continued well being, in spite of difficult transitions.

3. Make sure the children understand that they were not the cause of the divorce.

4. Give clear and definite statements of mutual love and acceptance. Be prepared to back this up with actions such as hugs, interest in their world, and a listening ear.

5. Let them know that they can't get their parents back together. Encourage a realistic view of what life will be like after the divorce.

6. Expect that you will have to reinforce this information by opening discussions with your children about the divorce at regular intervals throughout their lives.

Chapter 9

Restructuring the Family

"My whole world was turned upsidedown when my parents broke up. My mom took my brother and I away from our home in order to live with our grandparents for a few months. After that we moved into this louzy apartment with no furniture. I had to attend a school that I used to make fun of. They were our rivals in sports, and the kids all seemed like drugees. Now I'm in this school, trying to make friends. It's like my worst nightmare come true.

My parents are always arguing about stupid stuff, mostly money and when my brother and I are coming over to see dad. I get tired of being in the middle of it. My mom tells me to ask dad for the support check when I see him. Then my dad starts yelling at me about how he'd send the check if 'your mother would let me see you guys when she is supposed to.'

I hate it when my parents talk to each other, because they always fight. But when they're not talking, I end up having to send messages back and forth."

—a sixteen year old boy.

Restructuring a home and a family is always difficult and stressful. When you add the grief and trauma of a divorce, you have the makings of an explosive situation. The purpose of this chapter is to provide guidelines as to how to make these changes with the least turmoil and emotional harm to the participants. Granted, one can never eliminate all of the negative consequences, or even their own mistakes, however, there is much that you as a parent can do to smooth the transition.

Here are some of the more prevelant problem areas in the transition from married life to single parenting.

Custody and Visitation

Other than money issues, I'm sure there is no other issue which is more troublesome or emotionally charged than the custody and visitation rights of each parent. It will not be our focus to discuss the different types of arrangements, and which one would work best in your situation, because there are too many variables involved. For information on your options, I encourage you to talk with a lawyer, or a divorce mediation specialist. Each State has it's own laws as well as trends, which vary according to the views of the judges who oversee such cases. You need to be advised by someone who is familiar with the system, and the way it works in your specific area.

However, as a psychologist, there is much that I can say about the emotional side of the custody and visitation battle; the first of which would be to not make it a battle. Remember, the more you can resolve amicably among yourselves, the more you will save in money, time, wear and tear on your nerves, and damaging effects to your children. I can't tell you how many times I have heard stories like Lori's. "My husband and I fought over who would get the children for almost five years. It started out bad, but only got worse with each new round of hearings. By the time we were done, we had used every possible devious tactic and called each other every name in the book. Of course, the children heard it all and the only winners were the lawyers. Our legal fees were over $40,000, which was more than we had tried to split bctwccn us some five years earlier."

Whenever I have a divorcing parent tell me that they want to fight the other parent in order to "come out on top", I feel compelled to tell them that *there are no winners in a divorce*, except perhaps for the lawyers. If you think that you are going to fight your particular case until you finally "win", please rethink what you are doing. You are not going to win. You will merely run out of resources and energy, at which point, you will probably compromise to a position which you probably could have obtained much earlier at half the expense.

Now that I have made an absolute statement, let me give you the exception. In cases of abuse or extreme misconduct on the part of the other parent, you need to "fight" for the rights of your children. Standing up for your own rights is something that I encourage all parents to do, but it is not worth battling the other parent, unless you or your children are in some type of physical or emotional danger. Fortunately this is the exception, rather than the rule.

Since you are not the most objective person to judge whether or not your case falls into the "extreme" category, I would encourage you to seek third party objectivity, from a neutral advisor. You need to recognize that your friends and relatives are usually bias in your favor, and your lawyer may tend to advocate an adversarial position for obvious reasons.

Here are some other guidelines in regard to custody and visitation rights.

1. Set up a good, workable visitation arrangement as soon as the separation occurs. This will help the child adjust to a new rou-

tine, while assuring continuity with both parents. This also paves the way for a more smooth settlement of the "official agreement". Keep the visitation consistent so that children know what to expect and when they will see the other parent. When unscheduled changes occur, let your children know as soon as possible.

2. With teenagers, flexibility is needed because of their busy schedules and outside activities. Both parents should respect the teens wishes, but not at the expense of the relationship with the other parent. For example, if your teen is planning to work on weekends, this must be decided and arranged in consultation with both parents, since it tends to greatly affect the relationship with the non-custodial parent.

3. Holidays need to be planned well in advance, and then explained to the children. Don't wait until the week before Christmas to talk with the other parent about how they are to be handled. This leads to undue stress for the parents and the child, at a time when you need it the least. Older children and teens may be consulted as to their wishes for the holidays, but once again, the final decision must be the parents'.

4. Unless your children are preschoolers, you should consult with them about the visitation arrangement. This is particularly true of teenagers. Even though you ask them their

opinion, make sure they understand that the final decision is up to the parents, and will not be decided by the children. Keep in mind your child's tendency to tell you what they think you want to hear. Therefore, you should expect that they will say one thing to you, and something else to the other parent. Don't embarrass them or punish them for this. They desperately want the love and loyalty of both parents. Use their wishes as input into your final decision.

5. If a court case becomes inevitable, try to keep the children out of it. If their testimony is crucial, see if it can be handled in the judges chambers, through a court appointed psychologist, or via video tape. Don't force a courtroom confrontation which will compel the child to testify for or against one of their parents.

6. Keep the communication lines open between you and the other parent. Keep all discusions of changes in the arrangements and any money issues, between the parents. Don't pass messages through the children. Try to have these discussions over the phone, when the kids are not around. That way if they become unavoidably "heated", your children will not be subject to the disagreement. Don't wait until the other parent comes to pick up or drop off the children to say, "Oh, by the way . . .". As you know, this leads to disagreements which the children can't help but wit-

ness. (If you have a particularly amicable relationship, you may have no problem with last minute changes.)

7. When the children are back with you, encourage them to talk about their time with the other parent, unless you find that you cannot listen without reacting. Don't pump them for specific information, such as dating relationships, or how "their mother" is spending her money. You know the motivation behind these questions, and you also know what that information does to you. Ask, "Did you guys have fun with your father this weekend?", and then be prepared to bite your tongue when they talk about how much fun it was or even how nice his new girlfriend is. This is extremely difficult for you, but for the sake of your children, encourage their honest expression of this significant part of their life.

If you find that you cannot listen to it without reacting, then be honest enough with your children to say, "It hurts me to hear this right now. I want you to have fun with your dad, and maybe someday we will be able to talk all about it, but for right now maybe we shouldn't." Then find ways to work on your own adjustment so that you can later encourage your children to share all areas of their lives, especially their relationship with the other parent, and perhaps a step-parent.

8. Both parents should set aside time alone, with each child. This gives them opportunity

to create special bonds, and to talk on a deeper level than is possible when all children are constantly together. This has proven to be an important factor in the building of a strong sense of security and a healthy self image.

9. Avoid being a "Disneyland Daddy" or a "Magic Mountain Mommy". Parents who do not normally live with the children tend to avoid the normal patterns of a realistic home environment. They want to make sure the children have a good time when they come to visit, so they may eat out frequently, do special things at every visit, and "fudge" on the rules regarding bedtime, homework, etc. In order to decrease the instability and competition between the parents, they should strive to provide the same stable and consistent discipline that is expected of the custodial parent. Although "special events" are nice, the majority of the time should be part of a daily routine, similar to what they do in the other home. Avoid presents or treats which seem like relationship bribes. Focus on building the relationship with your children through open communication and time spent doing everyday tasks.

10. Each child needs to feel the continued love of both parents, and that each parent encourages their relationship with the other. Ready access to the departed parent, by phone and in person is necessary. *You* will benefit if you help your child accept and love the other

parent, even when the other parent doesn't do the same.

Child Support and Alimony

Once again, our purpose here is not whether or not you should receive alimony, or how much child support you should get. You need to have that discussion with your lawyer or mediator. Rather, we want to discuss how these payments, (actually, the lack of these payments) effect your children. The rule is that all fathers (assuming dad is the non-custodial parent) will make their child support payment on time, and that if there is alimony due, it will be paid on time also. In reality, however, we know that not all payments are on time, and that many fathers make no payments at all. Whenever this occurs, the children are inevitably effected.

Unless the father is unemployed or on the verge of bankruptcy, his resistance to keep his financial obligation is ususally the result of unresolved anger or resentment toward the mother. Even though the father swears he loves his children, he may resist fulfilling his obligation toward them in order to make a point. Unfortuately, the children suffer because of this decision. Not only are their financial needs being neglected, but the father is contributing to a hostile atmosphere for the children at home. Their mother is placed under undo strain, and inevitably will tell the children that "I'm sorry I can't get you those sneakers, but your father hasn't sent the support check."

Witholding payments is many times the result of a conflict over visitation arrangements. Fathers tell me that they are not going to pay because their former spouse does not send the children when she is supposed to. Predictably, the mother then tells me that she doesn't send the kids on time, because of the father's sporadic payments. This never ending "catch-22" has no winners, and the children end up suffering the most. For the sake of your children, *don't do it!*

Child support and alimony are legal obligations, and have nothing to do with your children. You need to keep your obligations regardless of your relationship with your children or your former spouse. If you are not happy with the arrangement, then take it up *privately* with the other parent. If that does not resolve your concerns, then take it to your lawyer or mediator. Don't resort to punishing your children for your inability to get along with their mother.

On the otherhand, (just in case you mom's thought you were getting off easily) just because your former spouse doesn't make their payments on time, or doesn't even make them at all, you have no right to block their relationship with their children. The same principles apply. The father's visitation rights are a legal obligation, and are critical to your child's healthy adjustment to divorce (assuming he is not abusive). Therefore, his non-payment must be taken up with him first, and then taken to the legal authorities. Fortunately, the courts are beginning to take these matters more seriously, and have started cracking down on "dead beat dads". Many, however, continue to fall through the cracks in the system.

But what do we tell the children? In the beginning, as little as possible. Children, and even teens should be kept out of the financial arrangements and disagreements. However, when the problem pursists, such as when no payment has been made in several months, then you may have to tell the children the truth. Let them know that you don't want them to get involved in the dispute, but that "because your father has not made several payments, we will all have to tighten our belts a bit". Let them know that you want them to continue having a good relationship with their father.

I know that this advice is hard to swallow when you're in the midst of the financial crisis; or when you can't begin to see any redeeming qualities in the other parent. So let me remind you of the long term effects of

divorce on children, and once again point out
that a continued relationship with both parents is crucial to the psychological well-being
of your children. Try to focus on, "What is the
underlying issue in this dispute?"; and "How
can I resolve it without putting my children
in the middle?".

Your Child and the School

Mrs. Graham didn't want the school to find
out that her husband had left. She had her two
children, Martha and Michael, in a private
Christian school. She was afraid that the
school's conservative philosophy would preju-
dice the teachers and administrators against
her children. Or that if teachers knew, they
would watch her children too closely, and almost "look for trouble" in her kids.

The problem with Mrs. Graham's cautious
attitude is that her fears are unfounded, and
may be depriving the children of significant
help. As a school psychologist in Philadelphia, I consulted with teachers and prin-
cipals in over 20 public and private schools. It
was my experience that teachers were sensitive and compasionate when they became
aware of a student's struggles. They were
harder on children when they started falling
behind or missing assignments with no apparent reason. But in the case of divorce, teachers
would make allowances for the child's dis-

tractability, academic regression, emotional withdrawal, or hostility.

Teachers have a variety of resources available to them to help children. Books, tapes, videos, and counselors are usually at the disposal of your children, as long as the school is aware of your need. The school might be holding support groups for children of divorce, or know were they are being held in your community. The bottom line is that you won't know this unless you inform the school of what is going on at home.

If your child is a teenager, they probably have a variety of teachers, and most likely would not appreciate your contacting all of them. In this case, a call to the guidance counselor or advisor may be most helpful. If it is a large school, there is little the counselor will probably do unless they have a special program, or unless your child comes in for help. Older children are more influenced by their peer group, and therefore, will tend to talk with friends far more than they will talk with teachers or a counselor. Encourage the peer interaction, especially with other children who have been through the same thing. They can become a trememdous help to each other. (This is a major premise of the "Kids in the Middle" programs that we conduct; kids helping other kids.) However, you may need to correct distorted peer feedback from time to time, especially if your child's friends are immature or hostile. Try to be aware of the kinds of support your child is receiving from other kids.

Changes at Home

"When my family got a divorce, my whole world changed forever. We moved to a new home, new school district, a new church, and all new friends. I don't know what hurt the most, missing my dad, or missing my friends from my old neighborhood and school."

This quote from an eleven year old girl illustrates the child's need for stability amidst the turmoil. There will always be changes to face. Some of these changes may even be good, especially over the long term. Yet when separation or divorce first occurs, it is helpful if you can keep the changes to a minimum. If you have to move, try to stay in the same school district, or the same social group. Your friendships may evolve toward more single people, and fewer married couples, but try to make this transition gradual and smooth.

As parents get together in single's groups and social clubs, it is inevitable that the children will socialize as well. This can result in positive new relationships with other kids who have been through similar life changes. This reinforces the fact that "I am not alone", and allows the child the opportunity to talk to other kid's about their concerns. Nevertheless, as a parent you can't push these new friendships too quickly. Encourage the child to continue their long term friendships, while allowing new relationships to develop naturally.

Keep the household schedule, responsibilities, and discipline as consistent as possible. If you did not work before, and now have to work, your schedule will obviously change. Sit down with your children, explain the need for the changes, and then let them know what they can expect for the future. It is most important that your children know that you want to be with them, that you want to care for them, but that the changes force everyone to take on more responsibilities. For example, "I have to go back to work in order to help pay the bills. This means that I won't be here when you get home from school. I would love to be here for you, fix your snack and hear all about your day. But unfortunately you'll have to wait until I get home at 5:30. That means you'll have to fix your own snack, and you may even need to help set the table before I get home. What's important is that we work together and make our relationship even stonger than it was before".

Here are a few additional guidelines which should help you handle the changes at home.

1. Although increased responsibilities are inevitable, don't allow your kids to become hyper-responsible, taking on burdens and chores that they should not shoulder. Let your children remain children. No matter how ma-

turely they act, don't fool yourself into believing they can take on adult responsibilities. Boys are particularly susceptable to thinking "now that I'm the man of the house, I need to be here for mom". One boy just told me how he could not go away to school in the fall because his mom was going through a difficult time and would need a man around the house. Remember the "overburdened child syndrome"?

2. It is important that parents avoid confiding in their children as if they were a peer. This can happen when moms talk to their daughters about "what a tough life it is out there". Or when dad tells his son all about the women he's dating. Let your child remain a child.

As a parent, you want a close relationship with your children, but there must be some boundries in that relationship. If you have a problem with setting limits and boundries in relationships, or grew up in a home where boundries were confused, then you may be unconciously passing this on to your children. If this is the case, I encourage you to seek counseling for your own issues, so that you can create a healthier balance for your children.

3. Don't force your children to make choices that will create loyalty conflicts for them. For example, don't ask your children, "Who do you want to spend your birthday with, your mom or your dad?". This creates a

no win situation for your children. If they pick you, they hurt the other parent. And how can they tell you that they'd rather be with the other parent? It would be best to get their input by asking a neutral question like, "How would you like to spend the holiday?". If they neglect the other parent, you may want to suggest a compromise which includes both parents. This approach demonstates that you are sincere in your desire that they have a good relationship with the other parent, and discourages the child's tendency to tell you what they think you want to hear.

4. Encourage your child to keep their fond memories of the other parent. Many times, upon separation, parents do a "clean sweep" of the house, throwing away all pictures or momentos that remind them of the other parent. While I understand the sentiment, try to save a photo album or two for your children which will remind them of good times together. A special picture or momento beside their bed or in a wallet should also be suggested. Remember, if you suggest it, this gives the child permission to love the other parent. If you don't suggest it, your child may assume that "mom would hit the roof if she saw a picture of *him* around".

Special "Friends" and Step-parents

When one is trying to restructure the family, adding a new "friend" or a step-parent to the system is like throwing a monkey wrench into the works. These additions generally cause a whole new set of adjustments which take years to work through. If this happens while children are still adjusting to the trauma of divorce, generally within the first two years, all of the emotions can be intensified and acceptance can be much further away. Therefore, many therapists recommend that newly divorced people not get involved in intimate relationships for at least two years following their divorce. This not only helps you to make your adjustment to the divorce, but helps your children also.

This does not mean that you should avoid new friendships, or even relationships with the opposite sex. On the contrary, these friendships, assuming they are healthy, are vital to your recovery. (See Appendix for *Sex and Love When You're Single Again* by Tom Jones.) What you need to avoid is committed relationships with the opposite sex, and emotional entanglements which complicate the recovery process for you and your children. These "rebound relationships" rarely last, and most often lead to more pain for everybody involved. The statistics on remarriage show that when someone remarries within two years of their divorce, they have a greater than 80% chance of going through another divorce. Do you or your children need that? For those who wait for two years, however, the odds of "making it" increase to about 50%, which is the same percentage as for first time marriages.

Having given this advice, your reaction may be, "That's fine for me, but try telling that to the other parent. They're already involved with someone else and we're not even divorced yet!". Unfortuately, reality would dictate that your divorce was probably exaserbated by the involvement of "another party" in the life of at least one parent, and perhaps both. So now what do you do?

Many parents will use the existence of an illicit affair as an excuse to keep the children away from the other parent. While I do not condone the relationship, and understand the depth of your resentment and jealousy, once again, I must defer to the greater good of your children. As one "kid in the middle" put it:

My dad left my mom to live with his girlfriend. When dad asked if he could pick us up for a visit, my mom refused to let us go over, because she didn't agree with his lifestyle. We knew that what my dad had done was wrong, and in many ways we were really ticked at him. But he was still our father, and we still loved him. Mom not letting us go only created a bunch of mudslinging between my parents. I think I would have respected my mom a lot more if she had told us how she felt, and then allowed us to see him. Now my dad is married to his girlfriend, and our

relationship is still strained. I don't want to
do it, but sometimes I blame my mom for the
fact that I don't really have a relationship
with my dad.

Unfortunately, dating relationships have a
way of becoming an additional battleground
in the post-divorce experience. Besides being
used as an excuse for curtailing visitation,
other pitfalls exist for your children as you
move toward that "special relationship". Here
are a few additional guidelines as you seek to
include opposite sex relationships in your re-
structured family.

1. As the non-custodial parent, it would be
best if you did most of your socializing on
weekends when you do not have the children.
Parenting needs to be your first priority, and
particularly in the first few years of your re-
structured family, you need to give your children as much of your time as possible. Your
"dates" will generally be viewed as an intru-
sion into your relationship with your children. As one particlar person becomes
important, you will want to introduce that
person into your children's lives in a very
gradual, non-threatening way.

2. It is probably much harder for the
custodial parent to have a social life. Some
potential dates may be scared off by your children, and then there is the problem of the
time and energy that it takes to maintain a

social life. However, when the opportunity arises, you should not feel guilty about getting a babysitter, and enjoying a night out. A balance is needed between your right to privacy, and your need to be honest with the kids. Your children don't need to meet and approve of everyone you go out with, but you should not hide the fact that you are dating. Your children's trust is built when you are honest with them, even though they may not like your going out without them. Expect some acting out and jealousy of your time and attention.

3. Don't encourage your casual dates to get close to your children. A positive male role model is *not* a series of men that you happen to date. This only confuses your children and reinforces the fact that relationships are not permenant. This adds to their insecurity. While teens are more understanding of temporary relationships, they too are not helped by your pushing your new "friends" on them. Integrate your opposite sex friends into your children's lives' only as they become an important part of yours. Allow the relationship to develop at its own pace, never pushing your children into an artificial acceptance.

4. Avoid the temptation to ask your children about the other parents' new friends. This puts your children in the position of a spy, and creates additional loyalty conficts. If they volunteer the information, try to show

little reaction. Encourage your children to treat your friends, and your ex-spouse's friends with respect. Don't allow the dating relationship to become a source of conflict.

5. If your children ask you questions about your dating relationships give them honest answers without personal details. For example, "Do you love Mr. So-and-so?", should be answered as honestly as you can without giving information about the depth of your relationship, or your plans for the future. That should wait until you are ready to take definate steps.

If your child asks, "Do you and Mr So-and-so kiss?", you should answer honestly without making a big deal out of it. Give no details, however, about your physical relationship.

Once these relationships progress to a point where it looks like a remarriage is iminent, you need to have a discussion with your children similar to the one outlined in Chapter Eight, when you were contemplating separation or divorce. Out of courtesy to your former mate, you may want to forewarn him/her before you tell the kids, so that he/she can begin to prepare themselves emotionally. Let's face it, remarriage of either spouse is a difficult transition for both the children and the parents.

Psychologically speaking, this is a big hurdle for the children. It is one which, 1) ends the fantasy that my parents might get back together, 2) triggers the fear that the new spouse will take away the love my parent has for me, and 3) creates anxiety about whether or not I will get along with this intruder in our family.

For the parent getting married, it finally closes one chapter in their life, and opens the door of new challanges and opportunities. For the parent remaining single, there is the feeling of being left behind; the anxiety of wondering "if I'll ever be able to move on like that".

As everyone makes the necessary adjustments, the anxiety that grips your children more and more is the feeling that, "now that dad has a new wife, he will have even less love and less time for me". This can be particularly threatening if the new marriage includes children. The blending of families is filled with so many complexities that it needs to be the subject of another book. For our purposes, a general review is in order.

In the 90's, one third of all children will spend at least some time with a step-parent before their eighteenth birthday. It is estimated that by the year 2000, the blended family will be the most common type of family in this Country. Yet researchers estimate that it takes an average of five years to successfully blend a family. For most of you getting remarried, your children will probably move out of the house before the necessary transitions are completed.

I have two close friends who were both in long term relationships which were moving toward marriage. They both chose to postpone their decision because they had teenagers at home. Rather than go through the difficulties of blending a family, both couples decided to wait until the children were out of the house before they got remarried. I'm not saying that you should do the same, I merely want to point out that this "blending" is more difficult than most people realize. One of my friends explained their decision this way.

> I know of over twenty remarried couples, all with teenagers in their blended families. I can't name one family who hasn't had major difficulties with their children after the marriage. I just decided that I didn't want to do that to my kids, so I've posponed my own remarriage for another two years. By then my youngest will leave for college.

A mother of a blended family described the following interaction between her teenage son and her new husband.

> Before I married Jim, he and my son Paul were like best friends. I was so excited because I thought that now, after thirteen years

of being by ourselves, Paul was going to have a father figure. The strangest thing happened though. As soon as we got back from the honeymoon, I noticed my son acting a little strange around Jim. Within a few weeks they were barely speaking, and now, after three years of marriage, Paul and Jim can't even look at each other without getting in a fight. I don't know what happened when Jim and I married, but something obviously clicked off for my son.

This example is not unlike many of the stories that I have heard from step-parents who are horrified by what happens when they try to blend a family. It never seems to be easy, and the way everyone gets along before the wedding does not seem to be a very good indication of what to expect after the wedding. In fact, it is not at all unusual for the children to push you toward marrying Mr. So-and-so, and then to create havoc after the wedding, saying they never really liked him.

If you are thinking about a remarriage, I would recommend getting a book which deals specifically with remarriage and step-parenting issues. (See Appendix) But for a general review of some of the issues you will face, here are a few guidelines.

1. The potential step-parent needs to be introduced to the children in a gradual and natural way. In the beginning, fun outings are best since they reduce the tension of "making

conversation". Once the initial transitions are over, however, natural family activities are best.

2. Don't expect instant rapport between your children and the new step-parent. These relationships take time, usually many years. If the relationship seems to go well from the beginning, expect a strained transition later.

3. Younger children usually adjust more quickly to a step-parent than do older children and teenagers.

4. The step-parent should try to observe the family customs and transitions, including giving the children gifts on special occasions. Be careful to not overdo the gift giving since children will tend to view this as a bribe.

5. Don't push your children to participate in your wedding. They may feel intense pressure to be loyal to the other parent. Let them know of your plans, and tell them that you would like for them to take part, but that you will let them decide for themselves. Then give them several weeks, if possible, to decide.

6. If the new step-parent does not have children, they need to educate themselves about childhood development and parenting. Don't assume it will come naturally. You are taking on a big commitment, and need to prepare yourself, particularly in the area of step-parenting.

7. Don't expect your children to love or

respect their step-parent as much as they do their biological parent. This is unrealistic, and sets the step-parent up for tremendous disappointment.

8. Don't force your children to call the new step-parent "Mom" or "Dad". Find out what they would prefer, and then try to compromise on a name or nickname that is acceptable to everyone, including your former spouse. (Yes, even after your remarriage, the lines of communication need to stay open.)

9. Continue to spend individual time with each of your children, and constantly remind them of your undiminished love for them. Keep in mind the child's fantasy that with each new person or child in your life, you will have less love for them. This is particularly strong if there is a step-child about the same age as your own child, or if there is a new baby born into the blended family.

10. While your children need to respect and listen to your new spouse, you need to remain their primary disciplinarian. Younger children can take correction from their step-parent more easily than older children and teenagers. Therefore, it is unfair to the step-parent for you to expect them to take on the major disciplinary role.

11. Children generally try to play one parent against the other, but this is particularly intense in a step-parent relationship. Try not to get sucked into this "divide and conquer"

stategy. Avoid taking sides with your children or your spouse. Instead, discuss the matter privately with your spouse and then come back and tell the children *your* decision. Remember, they will take it best if it comes from you, their parent.

12. It is important for you and the step-parent to keep in mind that intense feelings of anger and resentment are normal in the blended family, especially among the teen-agers. Try not to personalize the anger and respond in kind. You are probably bearing the brunt of years of perceived betrayal and disappointment. Be as patient and compassionate as you can be, knowing that this is a very difficult transition for everyone. A transition which statistically will last five years.

If you are parenting as a single, and your former spouse is remarrying, you will also have adjustments to make. Adjustments in your own attitudes, and adjustment with your children, as they report their feelings toward the new "creature" in their lives. It is probably a no win situation for you. If they love their new step-parent, you will feel "replaced"; and if they don't like their new step-parent, you will have to hear the weekly reports of how "she did this . . . , and she did that . . .".

Here are a few guidelines intended to help you and your children cope with these changes.

1. If you can't be accepting of your former

spouse's remarriage, at least try to stay as neutral and emotionally uninvolved as possible. If you are really struggling with the whole issue, you probably need to talk with a counselor or advisor about your feelings. It will effect your children's adjustment if you continue to have strong feelings about these changes.

2. Give your children permission to attend or participate in the wedding. Forbidding them will only hurt their relationship with *you* in the long run.

3. As hard as it might be for you to accept, you need to have at least a casual relationship with your former mate's new spouse. You will probably need to talk with him/her on the phone from time to time, and it really doesn't help the children if they see you snarling at each other every time you speak.

4. Give your children permission to talk about the times at the other parent's house. Listen to their stories about the other partner and the other children, but try not to make any judgements, or offer your opinion. Try to remain detatched when they complain about, or praise the step-parent. Stay out of what goes on in the other household, unless you have good reason for significant concern, such as "they don't feed us over there". Then, don't assume that it's true. Try to take it up calmly with your former spouse. Only involve the step-parent if you find that you get along bet-

ter with him/her than you do with your ex-spouse.

CHAPTER SUMMARY

In this chapter we have looked at some common areas of contention for single parents, and then presented some practical guidelines for helping your children over some of these difficult huddles. The following is a brief summary of some of these guidelines:

Increases Impact of Divorce	**Lessens Impact of Divorce**
1. Children are involved in visitation and custody squabbles.	1. Parents work out custody and visitation arrangement cooperatively.
2. Children are asked to choose between the parents.	2. Parents help children avoid loyalty conflicts by encouraging the relationship with the other parent.
3. Parents use the children to send messages.	3. Parents keep lines of communication open.
4. Parents become	4. Parents spend

too busy or distracted from their children.

5. Parents use the children and money as leverage to get what they want.

6. Parents isolate themselves and their children.

7. Parents expect the children to take the place of the missing parent.

8. Parents deny feelings and do not facilitate discussion with children.

9. Parents push children into relationships with a series of

quality time with each child

5. Parents keep money issues separate and away from the children.

6. Parents seek resources and support from a variety of settings, including church, school, family.

7. The child remains a child, even though increased responsibilities may be necessary.

8. Parents allow children to grieve.

9. Parents provide stable adult relationships with relatives

dating partners.

10. A remarriage before the children have had time to adjust to the divorce.

11. Parents maintain angry, bitter feelings.

12. Parents speak negatively about the other parent in front of the children.

13. Absent parent looses contact with the children.

and family friends.

10. Giving your children at least two years of adjustment before bringing a potential step-parent into their lives.

11. Parents recover and move on in a healthy new lifestyle.

12. Parents show and express respect for one another.

13. Absent parent maintains consistent contact with children.

Chapter 10

Parenting as a Single

"As a single parent of two preschool boys, I found my life going through an overwhelming set of changes. At first, I was too depressed to be of any good to anyone, including my boys. But as I moved along, I became determined that I was going to overcome my circumstances. That led me into my "superwoman" role, where I tried to do everything by myself. I took a full time job, arranged day care for the boys, ran the home, and tried to maintain a social life. I wanted to take the place of their missing father, but what I found was that I was becoming more and more frustrated, and the boys were usually mad at me. What a terrible feeling!

Now I'm just trying to be a decent mother. I no longer need to be superwoman. I don't even have to be good. I'm settling for doing the best I can, and spending whatever time I can with the boys. It's like I wanted 100% before, and now I'm settling for 75%. But at

least I might preserve my sanity this way, and who knows, maybe I'll even enjoy a few days."
                    —a 32 year old single mother.

Even though the preceding quote seems a little gloomy, it is a fairly accurate portrayal of how most single parents feel at least sometime in their lives. There is a sense that "I can't do it all myself", and "What do I really have to look forward to". There is no question that parenting as a single is an extremely challenging task, especially if you have little or no support from the other parent. Yet I know of many single parents who not only make it on their own, but appear to be happy, fulfilled, and are raising children who are very well adjusted. In this, our last chapter, we will look at ways to help you become more effective as a single parent; not only at raising your children, but also at enjoying the life that you have.

Two of the keys for successful single parenting that we want to focus on in this chapter, are the way that you raise your children, and your own attitude toward your circumstances. In the first half of the chapter we will discuss the "parenting" key, and then we will conclude with the ways in which your own attitude toward your circumstances effect the entire single parenting process.

Keys for Parenting as a Single

Once again, it is true that an entire book could be written on this topic alone. Therefore, what I will have to focus on, is an overview of the parenting issues. In addition, I will provide a list of other resources which might be helpful to you, if you would like to look more closely at a particular parenting skill.

Parenting as a single is not a whole lot different than parenting in general. Both require loving discipline, guidance, modeling, nurturing, teaching, and a full range of emotional supports. The greatest difference for the single parent is twofold; 1) your children tend to be more emotionally needy because of their sense of loss, and 2) you don't have the additional support of second parent who can share your decisions and frustrations. Therefore, you need to focus on a few critical skills that you can commit yourself to work on. Here are some of the most critical areas.

I. *Provide a loving environment for your children.*

Everyone would agree that providing your children with a loving environment is one of the most important gifts you can give to your children. However, many would disagree as to what a loving environment entails. Should we be firm, or compassionate; foster independence, or reliance on the family; give in to their wishes, or force them to "do without". These are all questions which probably have different answers depending on the circumstances, and the personality of your child. The important point is that you assure your children of your unconditional love for them.

Unconditional love for a child of divorce must come in the form of constant reassurance of your love and commitment to their well being. They need to know that you will be there for them and that they are a top priority, even though you have additional responsibilities that require your time. They need to see concrete expressions of that love during the good times and the bad. In other words, they need to see that you love them just as much on their good days, as you do on their worst.

Practical expressions of that love should include the following:

1. Verbal reassurance of *specific* things that you like about each child.

2. Physical contact with your child which includes hugs, kisses, back scratches, etc. (I still remember my mom waking me up on school days by gently scratching my back.)

3. Notes and cards that express pleasure with something they have done, or something

you like about their personality. (This is particularly helpful for the non-custodial parent to do.)

4. Spending individual time with each child. Finding a hobby or activity that you can share with them alone.

5. Actively listening to your child. Focus on them and what they are saying. Stop what you are doing and give them good eye contact. Do not give advice, or simplistic answers, but try to view the information through their eyes.

6. (For the non-custodial parent) Frequent phone calls during the week which focus on them and their day. Also, giving them a number where you can be reached at almost any time. They need to be assured that they have easy access to you when they feel they need to talk about something.

No one is capable of displaying unconditional love at all times. However, if this is your goal, then you need to also be able to ask for forgiveness when you "lose it" with your kids. If you grew up in a home that was less than loving, then you might have particular difficulty expressing this love to your children. For a more in depth look at learning how to love your children, I would recommend the following books: *How to Really Love Your*

Child, by Ross Campbell, *The Art of Loving*, by Eric Fromm, and *Unconditional Love*, by John Powell. (See Appendix).

II. *Rebuild trusting relationships.*

One of the casualties of a divorce, is the ability to trust again, at least in the immediate aftermath. This is just as true for the children as it is for adults. As a parent, it is primarily *your* responsibility to rebuild your child's trust, since you are probably the most influential adult in their lives. You may also be the target of their distrust, if you were the one who left, or if you are perceived as having betrayed the family in some way.

Rebuilding trust takes time, but above all, requires complete honesty from you. This is demonstrated in the way you explain divorce to your children, whether or not you are willing to admit your own mistakes, how honest you are with your feelings, and whether or not you keep your word to the children. In an effort to compensate the children for the losses experienced in the divorce, some parents compound the mistake by making promises to the children that they are not sure they can keep. The vacations, the trips to Disneyworld, and the extravagant toys, do not tell the children that you love them, but rather, more often then not, are reinforcement of the belief that mom or dad can't be trusted.

Even if you got away with minor unfulfilled promises before the divorce, what you must now realize is that now your life is under a microscope. Your children are testing to see if they can trust you again. Therefore, you must take special care to measure your words before you speak.

These promises include the negative ones too. If you tell your children, "If I hear you whine one more time, I'll send you to your room for a month". Don't say it unless you can follow through on your word! This might seem like a minor infraction, for which we have all been guilty. But now, more than ever, it is imperative that you think before you speak.

Think about the following statements:

"If you do that one more time, I'll kill you!"

"If you don't clean up your plate, you won't eat for a week."

"If you don't get in the car right now I'll never take you to grandma's again."

Besides the fact that you shouldn't make such harsh statements, think about the message that these words convey to your children regarding their ability to trust you again. Yet I know that we've all sent these messages, or not followed through on a commitment merely because it slipped our minds. When we become aware of these mistakes, it is important that we, once again, speak the truth as lovingly as we can.

"I'm sorry I said that. Mommy didn't really mean that she wouldn't feed you for a week. I only said that out of frustration. You need to finish your meal, or you won't get any dessert."

"I know daddy said he would take you fishing this weekend, but I forgot that I had to get the car inspected. That was my fault for not remembering. I know that you're disappointed, but I'm sure we will be able to go some other time. How about if we try. . . ."

III. *Provide firm, yet loving discipline.*

Another casualty in many divorcing families, is a continued level of loving discipline (assuming it was formerly present). As you lose touch with your children, or lose the energy to keep up with their shenanigans, many parents take the easy way out, which is to give in or react in haste. Yet consistent discipline is key to the child of divorce feeling secure, loved.

It is not within the scope of this book to cover the full range of disciplining techniques, therefore, I will review a few guidelines, and then recommend some books.

1. "Make the punishment fit the crime". This takes a great deal of wisdom, and no one can be there to tell you how to handle each new situation, but don't over-react to minor in-

fractions, and take seriously the mistakes which carry long term implications. The way this is played out in many homes is for parents to let things slide until they've had enough. Then they react with "the back of their hand", or a threat that everyone knows they will not follow through on.

Logical consequences make the most sense, and also teach valuable lessons, such as:

"If you don't put away your toys, I'll have to take them away for a couple of days."

"If you don't turn off the Nintendo now, you won't be allowed to play with it tomorrow."

"Since I don't like to see you act that way, why don't you sit in the other room until you're done pouting."

The consequences to each situation require thought and patience. This means that you need to stay calm, and not react in the anger of the moment. The easiest thing to do is not always the best.

2. "Pick your battle grounds". This is a simple phrase to express the need for you to decide which areas are important enough to "battle" over. This is particularly true of teenagers. Since discipline takes a lot of thought and energy, you may decide not to battle over "cleaning up every bite on your plate", or whether your daughter can wear make-up to school. You need to decide in advance which

issues are important, and on which you need to show some latitude.

3. Distinguish between accidents, disobedience, and defiance. Even though accidents may be devastating to you personally, you don't want to deal with them as harshly as disobedience or defiance. For example, if my daughter spills her juice on my computer and ruins it, I'm going to be very upset. (Especially if I'm at the end of a chapter that I hadn't "saved" to the disk yet.) Her seeing how upset I am may be punishment enough. In fact, I'd probably end up hugging her and assuring her that, "It's okay, I realize that it was an accident".

However, if I tell her to sit in the kitchen and drink her juice, and instead, she walks into my office and spills her juice, now I need to punish her for disobedience. Perhaps sitting her in her chair for a while would be just penance, even though my anger at the moment might want me to do more.

The most serious infraction, however, would be defiance. That would be evidenced in my daughter looking me right in the eye, and pouring the juice on my computer, right after I told her to take her juice back to the kitchen. For this, a young child could be spanked, or restricted to her room. An older child might have to work in order to replace the computer they ruined (logical consequence of their action).

As you can see from the example, the result is the same. My computer is ruined. The difference which needs to be distinguished is; was it an accident, disobedience, or defiance?

4. Explain to your children the difference between your feelings toward them and your feelings about their behaviors. In other words, tell your children, "I love you, but I don't like the way you are behaving".

Remember when your parents used to say "This is going to hurt me more than it will hurt you", just before they spanked you? Even though that used to drive us crazy at the time, I believe the message behind the words is that "because I love you, I have to do this; but it hurts me too."

Think about the following statements, and how they should be said.

"You're stupid", might become "I know you are very capable, but the way you're acting right now isn't very smart".

"Shut up!" could be stated, "I want to listen to you, but could you please stop talking right now so that I can think".

"I hate it when you do that!" might need the minor modification to, "I love you, but I don't like it when you do that".

These changes seem obvious in the calm reality of the present, but they take great willpower and thought when you reach the height of your frustration. I guess that's why people say, "Parenting is hard work!".

Some books which take a closer look at issues of disciplining your children are, *Dare to Discipline*, *The Strong Willed Child*, by James Dobson, and *The Key To Your Child's Heart*, by Gary Smalley. (See Appendix).

V. Foster healthy relationships.

As a single parent it is very important that you promote healthy role models for your children. This usually includes monitoring who they hangout with, finding positive opposite sex and same sex adult relationships, and providing some exposure to healthy, intact families. Here are a few guidelines to help you accomplish this.

1. Insist on meeting your childrens' friends. Even if they are teenagers, you are entitled to know who your children are hanging around with. Try to be friendly and open-minded toward all of them. Be very cautious about disapproving of any of their friends, since this can make the relationship even more important. Remember, you can't pick your children's friends. To even suggest a person can sometimes be the "kiss of death" for that relationship. Usually, the most you can do is to put your children in places where they will be in close proximity with a more desirable peer group. (church, the YMCA, clubs, civic groups, etc.)

2. Find adult role models for your child that will be a stable and reliable influence. This is especially important if your former mate does not provide that type of support. If the other parent is not very involved with your children, then a role model of the opposite sex is critical. This should be a family friend, a grandparent, an uncle; someone who they can count on being there for them over the long haul. *Not* a series of boyfriends or girlfriends who might be in and out of your life.

If it is a friend, then it is best when the person is primarily interested in helping your children, and not trying to get closer to you. If no one has shown a real interest in fulfilling this role, you might want to ask a friend or relative specifically to help out. They might not realize the need, and would be flattered that you asked.

3. Even though many of your friendships will evolve away from married couples and toward singles, it is important that you maintain relationships with some healthy married couples. It is good for both you and your children to observe some happily married couples, so that you don't lose your perspective. One teenager recently told me, "I don't know if I'll ever get married. I don't know of a single family where there hasn't been a divorce, or of one that isn't headed in that direction".

Another girl told me, "I'm real nervous

around men. I've never lived in a home with a man because my dad left when I was three. Whenever I'm around couples, I always check out the husband and wife to see how they act. I want to know what a normal family looks like for when I get married. That is, if that ever happens".

Again, times with relatives and friends who are married, both during holidays and when they're just doing their daily routine, can be a very important part of your child's development.

V. *Build a positive sense of self worth.*

No matter what your job, your most important responsibility is raising your children. And probably one of the greatest gifts that you can pass on to your children is a balanced self image. Of all of the problems that I face in counseling and in day to day contact with people, the most prevalent and pervasive is that of insecurity and poor self image. To some extent, we *all* struggle with this from time to time.

Each of us must ask, "What does our society value in a person, and what values do I reinforce in my home?" Unfortunately, in most settings, children see that they are valued primarily in four areas: beauty, brains, brawn, and bucks. Our society reflects these values in everything from advertising and cartoons, to who gets elected to the local school board or women's club.

If children are not good looking or smart, they often feel like failures and may be treated that way by classmates. This is particularly true for girls, who above all must look like a "Barbie Doll".

Boys on the other hand can get away with not being exceptionally handsome or smart, as long as they are good at sports, or are one of the strongest kids in the class.

The fourth area of value is one that we adults know well. Yet you may be surprised at how important money is to a child's popularity and standing with his peers. Our children must wear the right clothes, have the latest games and toys, and even have the correct label on their sneakers. Children are also keenly aware of who lives in the "right" neighborhoods, and whose parents are influential in the community.

If a child does not have at least one of the four ingredients —beauty, brains, brawn, or bucks—then he is destined to an uphill struggle in order to achieve acceptance in our society. One difficult truth that complicates this problem is that no matter how blessed we may be, there is always someone out there who is a little prettier, smarter, stronger, or

richer. No matter how many of the ingredients we do have, we will still struggle from
time to time with a negative self image.

Given these difficulties, how can I help to
develop a positive self image in my child? Let
me briefly describe some general guidelines,
and then recommend a few books which ex-
pand on this topic.

1. First and foremost, you need to love yourself before you can properly love others. If you
do not have a good self image, then your first
task is to get help for yourself, so that you can
model a positive self image to your children.

2. You need to counterbalance what their
peer group values. When your children are
with you, you need to show them a more
secure kind of love. One that is not based on
how they look or act, but one that values and
loves them all the time. As mentioned earlier,
show them a love that is unconditional.

3. Nurture your children with physical attention, and concrete expressions of love. Again,
be sure to mention specific things that you
like about each child.

4. Encourage your child to be open and honest with their feelings. Don't negate their feelings even when you disagree with them. For
example, "I'm sorry you feel like you're not
loved. I can understand how much that hurts.
But let me assure you that you are loved, . . .".

You need to be an example of open and honest communication.

5. Foster independence in your child. Remember, your goal is not to create obedient clones, but responsible adults. Therefore, you must encourage their decision-making and willingness to try things on their own, even when you think it might lead to failure. When they do fail, allow them to suffer the consequences, but then be there for them emotionally, encouraging them to try again.

Some additional guidelines can be found in the following books: *How to Really Love Your Child*, by Ross Campbell, *Hide and Seek*, by James Dobson, *The Key to Your Child's Heart*, by Trent and Smalley, and *Raising Positive Kids in a Negative World*, by Zig Zigler. (See Appendix)

VI. *Giving your children a sense of purpose or meaning in their lives.*

This is a parenting skill which is vastly overlooked, and yet is critically important for your child's healthy development. Children and adults *need* to have something in their lives which gives them meaning and purpose. For some it is their work, for others it may be in serving their fellow man, while others seek a personal relationship with God. Whatever your pursuit, you have probably come to find that living solely for "me and my needs", is an unfulfilling, selfish quest. Instead, many have found greater fulfillment when they live their lives for something beyond themselves.

One of the failures of the "Yuppie" generation was their pursuit of wealth and power, devoid of ethical considerations. King Solomon, one of the richest and powerful men of his time, said, "all that the world has to offer is a vain pursuit". As we teach our children how to make their way in this world, we must not forget that a faith or belief system should be part of the fabric of our lives.

I hear many parents almost apologize for what they believe. This sends a message to our children about how important our moral values are to us. I realize that many don't want to offend others, but with our children, I believe we have an obligation to present a firm set of values which tell us who we are, and why we are here. Young children will not understand these concepts, and your teenagers will rebel against them, so many parents ask, "Why bother?". The answer is one that you have heard before. Children may not understand it now, or may not want to hear it later, but the seeds you plant today will have a big influence on how they live as adults. Solomon puts it this way in the book of Proverbs, "Train up a child in the way he should go, and when he is old, he will not depart from it".

There are many things that you will want to teach your children as they grow up, but I believe the best way to teach a belief system, or your faith, is to live it. You obviously don't want to "preach it" without living it. That would only create an opposite reaction. If you don't have meaning or purpose in your own life, then obviously that needs to be settled first and foremost. For this, I would recommend the book *Power for Living*, by Jamie Buckingham. Free copies are available through the Fresh Start program. (See Appendix).

Your Attitude Toward Your Situation.

Let's shift our focus from our children to ourselves. Actually, we have come full circle in this book. In the first chapter, I mentioned the Serenity Prayer, and how important an attitude of acceptance toward the things that you cannot change can be in your recovery. I then went on to discuss the things that you can change, and how you can effect positive change for your children. Now, in this final section, we will take a closer look at how your attitude toward your circumstances can effect your entire life.

The parents' attitude about their situation has a large bearing on how they interact with their former spouse, how they relate with their children, and the speed at which their own recovery takes place. Let's contrast two situations.

Both Mrs. A and Mrs. B are suburban house-wives. Their husbands left them for younger women, as they were approaching their for-tieth birthdays. Both women were devastated by the loss, as were their children. Neither women were educated beyond their high school degrees, and neither have worked since getting married. Mrs. A views herself as a victim. She is angry with her ex, and boasts about giving him a hard time. She got full legal and physical custody of their three chil-dren, along with four years of alimony so that she could be trained for some type of new career. Presently, about two years after her divorce, Mrs. A is working as a receptionist for a little more than minimum wage. She has no plans for her vocational education because she says "I'm really not very good at anything. Besides", she explained, "I never wanted this divorce in the first place. I don't think I should have to work when I have three kids at home".

Mrs. A has very few social outlets, and many of her married friends are now drifting away from her. She is feeling more and more isolated, and tells her children about how un-fair all of this has been for her. Her children feel sorry for her, and feel guilty when they want to visit their dad. He has been sporadic in his visits, and late with many of his pay-ments, but as he puts it, "At least I'm still there for them when they need me".

Mrs. B, on the other hand, seems to be

doing a whole lot better. She went back to school, and now, two years later is well along in her Business Administration degree. She has already started her own small business, doing word processing out of her home. She also has physical custody of her two children, but she and her ex have joint legal custody. Mrs. B requested this arrangement because she knew that her husband would stay more involved in the kids' lives if he had some continuing input into their upbringing. As she put it, "I may not be married to him, but he is still their father. Even though he didn't turn out to be such a good husband, he was always a good father, and I believe he still is."

Mr. B feels very connected with his children, and they enjoy their visits with him. They feel good about leaving for his place, and good about telling mom all about their weekends, because they know that their mother encourages the relationship.

Mrs. B is also very involved socially. She has found a whole new support system, with friends who have been through similar life changes. Yet she still stays friendly with one or two of the married couples with whom she was formerly connected. Mrs. B has described her life in this way.

I wouldn't wish divorce on my worst enemy, but I wouldn't trade anything for what I have learned having gone through a divorce. I have more self confidence and feel more fulfilled now than I ever have. I never would have thought I could make it on my own while I was married, but now I know I can. I understand more about myself and other people, which I think has made me a better friend to my friends, a better parent to my kids, and a better overall person. Sure I get lonely sometimes, but there are worse things than being single and lonely, and one of them is to be in a bad marriage. Besides, now I have much stronger friendships. People that I know I can count on when I need a listening ear.

In our Fresh Start seminars we describe a poster that features a man with a funnel in his head, and a spicket where his nose should be. In the funnel is a bunch of lemons, and out of the spicket, lemonade is pouring into a pitcher. The caption reads, "When life gives you lemons, make lemonade".

This is a perfect illustration of how divorce effects our lives. We have all been given some lemons in our life. (Some of us married them.) Yet, in spite of these bitter experiences, we still have the ability to choose our own attitude toward our circumstances. Will we choose to become bitter; to squeeze those lemons and serve other people lemon juice? You know what happens when someone serves lemon juice. The sour taste turns people away. We alienate our friends, our children, and ourselves.

Or will we choose to add some sugar to that lemon juice and serve lemonade? The sugar that we all possess, is our own sweet disposition; the ability to forgive, to love, and to uplift others. When we add this to the bitter experiences of life, we find a perfect combination of sweet and sour, which attracts others, like lemonade on a hot and thirsty day.

Charles Swindoll, in his book, *Strengthening Your Grip*, (see Appendix) explains this concept as follows (p.205–206):

> The colorful, nineteenth-century showman and gifted violinist Nicolo Paganini was standing before a packed house, playing through a difficult piece of music. A full orchestra surrounded him with magnificent support. Suddenly one string on his violin snapped and hung gloriously down from his instrument. Beads of perspiration popped out on his forehead. He frowned but continued to play, improvising beautifully.
>
> To the conductor's surprise, a second string broke. And shortly thereafter, a third. Now there were three limp strings dangling from Paganini's violin as the master performer completed the difficult composition on the one remaining string. The audience jumped to its feet and in good Italian fashion, filled the hall with shouts and screams, 'Bravo! Bravo!' As the applause died down, the violinist asked the people to sit back down. Even though they knew there was no way they could expect an encore, they quietly sank back into their seats.

He held the violin high for everyone to see.
He nodded at the conductor to begin the en-
core and then he turned back to the crowd,
and with a twinkle in his eye, he smiled and
shouted, 'Paganini . . . . and one string!' After
that he placed the single-stringed
Stradivarius beneath his chin and played the
final piece on *one* string as the audience (and
the conductor) shook their heads in silent
amazement. 'Paganini . . . and one string!'
And, I might add, an attitude of fortitude.

Dr. Victor Frankl, the bold, courageous Jew
who became a prisoner during the Holocaust,
endured years of indignity and humiliation
by the Nazis before he was finally liberated.
At the beginning of his ordeal, he marched
into a gestapo courtroom. His captors had
taken away his home and family, his cher-
ished freedom, his possessions, even his
watch and wedding ring. They had shaved his
head and stripped his clothing off his body.
There he stood before the German high com-
mand, under the glaring lights being interro-
gated and falsely accused. He was destitute, a
helpless pawn in the hands of brutal, preju-
diced, sadistic men. He had nothing. No, that
isn't true. He suddenly realized there was one
thing on one could ever take away from
him—just one. Do you know what it was?

Dr. Frankl realized he still had the power to
choose his own attitude. No matter what
anyone would ever do to him, regardless of
what the future held for him, the attitude
choice was his to make. Bitterness or forgiveness. To give up or to go on. Hatred or
hope. Determination to endure or the paral-

ysis of self-pity. It boiled down to 'Frankl . . . and one string!'[1]

Words can never adequately convey the incredible impact of our attitude toward life. The longer I live, the more convinced I become that life is 10 percent what happens to us and 90 percent how we respond to it.

For you, the question remains, "What will *my* attitude be toward *my* circumstances?". Will it be bitterness, self-pity, and immobilization, as with Mrs. A; or will you choose forgiveness, hope, endurance, and determination, as Mrs. B described. What kind of music are you going to play on that one string of your's?

Now I know you're thinking, "Yeah but you don't understand how much I've been hurt". Or, "You can't imagine what a creep I was married to". Look again at the life of Victor Frankl. You could not have suffered as much as he. *Are you going to be a victim or a victor?* And before you answer that you'd rather remain in your self-pity, think about your children. Do you want *them* to overcome their circumstances? And what attitude would you like for them to choose? The research has demonstrated that the attitude of the parent, and especially the custodial parent, is the biggest predictor of the child's adjustment.

The title of this book is *Innocent Victims*. Yet that does not convey the attitude that you and your children need to adopt. Even though you have had some terrible things happen to you as a family, I believe there is still great hope. You *can* serve lemonade; and your children can serve lemonade too. It's your choice!

CHAPTER SUMMARY

In this, our final chapter, we have examined some of the most important keys for parenting as a single. Each parenting key included practical guidelines on how to implement them. They included:

1. Provide a loving environment for your child.
2. Rebuild trusting relationships.
3. Provide firm yet loving discipline.
4. Foster healthy relationships.
5. Build a positive sense of self worth.
6. Give your children a sense of purpose and meaning to their lives.

In the last section, we discussed the importance of your attitude toward your situation, and how that effects the recovery of you and your children. I believe that your decision to "play beautiful music" on whatever strings you have left, is the most important gift that you can pass on to your children—the truly innocent *"victors"* over divorce.

1. Dale Galloway, *Dream a New Dream*, Tyndale House, 1975, p.59.

Appendix

The following books are recommended readings available from Fresh Start Publications, which deal with specific issues surrounding divorce and single parenting. Any of these books or tapes can be ordered by calling our office at 1–800–882–2799 during regular business hours (E.S.T.). Please have your VISA or Mastercard ready if you would like to order by phone. Written requests should be sent to, Fresh Start, 751 N. Wayne Ave., Wayne Pa., 19087, Attn: Orders; with checks made payable to "Fresh Start". Discounts are available for orders over 10 books. Please allow 2–4 weeks for delivery and add $1.50 for shipping and handling. (Books marked with a * are most highly recommended.)

Adult Children of Divorce

Second Chances, Judith Wallerstein, Ticknor & Fields, 1989, $9.95.

The Adult Child of Divorce, Brisset & Burns, Thomas Nelson Publishing, 1991, $8.95.

Anger

Dance of Anger, Harriet Goldhor Learner, Harper & Row, 1985, $9.95.

Children's Books

These books are designed to be read with your children in order to promote discussion and healing from divorce.

The New Red Bike, Miner & Whiteman, Fresh Start Publications, 1990. A book to help children to realize that divorce was not their fault. Ages 4–8. $4.95.

The Mystery of The Midnight Scream, Gregg Miner, Fresh Start Publications, 1991. A book to help children realize that they are not alone in their grieving. Ages 5–10. $4.95.

Codependency

Codependent No More, Melody Beattie, Harper & Row, 1989, $9.95.

Beyond Codependency, Melody Beattie, Harper & Row, 1987, $9.95.

How To Break Your Addiction To A Person, Howard Halpern, Bantam, 1982, $4.95.

Depression

Getting Undepressed, Gary Emery, Simon & Schuster, 1988, $8.95.

Depression, Baker & Nester, Multnomah Press, 1983, $8.95.

Happiness Is A Choice, Minirth & Meier, Baker Books, 1978, $7.95.

Divorce Recovery

Through The Whirlwind, Bob Burns, Thomas Nelson Publishing, 1989, $8.95.

*Fresh Start Tape Series: Eight 60 minute audio tapes on recovery from divorce. $29.95.

Parenting

Dare to Discipline, James Dobson, Tyndale House, 1970, $8.95.

Hide or Seek: Building Your Child's Self Esteen, James Dobson, Revell Co., 1979, $7.95.

How to Really Love Your Child, Ross Campbell, Victor Books, 1982, $5.95.

Raising Positive Kids In a Negative World, Zig Ziglar, Oliver-Nelson, 1985, $14.95.

The Key To Your Child's Heart, Gary Smalley, Thomas Nelson, 1988, $8.95.

The Strong Willed Child, James Dobson, Tyndale House, 1978, $9.95.

Relationships

*Sex and Love When You're Single Again, Tom Jones, Thomas Nelson Publishing, 1990, $8.95.

Friends and Friendship, Jerry & Mary White, NavPress, 1982, $6.95.

Quality Friendships, Gary Inrig, Moody Press, 1981, $8.95.

*The Road Less Traveled, Scott Peck, Simon & Schuster, 1978, $11.95.

Dropping Your Guard, Chuck Swindoll, Word Books, 1983, $4.95.

Remarriage

How to Blend a Family, Carolyn Johnson, 1989, $8.95

Remarriage: Opportunity to Grow, Charles Cerling, Power Books, 1988, $6.95.

The Blended Family, Frydenger & Frydenger, Zondervan, 1985, $8.95.

Separation

Hope for the Separated, Gary Chapman, Moody Press, 1982, $6.95.

The Case Against Divorce, Diane Medved, Ivy Books, 1990, $4.95.

Spiritual Life

Power for Living, Jamie Buckingham, De-Moss Foundation, FREE!

Disappointment With God, Philip Yancy, Zondervan, 1988, $15.95.

Inside Out, Larry Crabb, NavPress, 1988, $12.95.

No Wonder They Call Him The Saviour, Max Lucado, Multnomah Press, 1986, $8.95.

Strengthening Your Grip, Charles Swindoll, Word Books, 1982, $4.95.